To Cath[...]
with m[...]
Christmas 1974
for
Sheena & Jimmy

PRESSED FLOWER
COLLAGES

AND OTHER IDEAS

"One Upmanship"

I get more pleasure in receiving the gift of a leaf than if I had been given a purse of gold!
My publisher, ever hopeful that I would create for him a soldier out of leaves, gave me the
gift of five large horse-chestnut leaves and a beech leaf hoping this would do the trick.
Instead, in one hour, I created these two rabbits, and also Farmer Barley Corn (page 70).
The crouching, timorous rabbit has only found four-leafed clovers while his friend has a
"five-leafer".

PRESSED FLOWER COLLAGES

AND OTHER IDEAS

PAMELA McDOWALL

LUTTERWORTH PRESS
GUILDFORD AND LONDON

First Published 1971
Second Impression 1972

ISBN 0 7188 18679

PRINTED IN GREAT BRITAIN BY EBENEZER BAYLIS AND SON, LIMITED
THE TRINITY PRESS, WORCESTER, AND LONDON

Contents

Three examples of how attractive a door finger-plate and two matchboxes can be made using pressed flowers. The finger-plate shows a Honeysuckle halliana reassembled in the form of a wild honeysuckle. The smaller matchbox is decorated with a pond primula, a daisy stalk and buds of montbretia, while the one on the right is created from buttercups, Heuchera sanguinea, a common daisy and wild brome grass.

Introduction

Pick for a purpose,
Press for a reason,
Whatever the month
The hobby's in season.

AND THIS SEEMS to be true! The winter months are ideal for using the pressed flowers gathered throughout the spring and summer for making not only pictures to decorate the walls, but smaller articles. Pressed flowers can decorate matchboxes, book-markers, calendars and note-book covers, as well as door finger-plates and table mats. Indeed, making and sending your very own "home-grown" decorated greeting card—in pressed flowers—is quite a novelty. Garden flowers as well as such wild flowers as clover, the common daisy, cow parsley and the lovely shiny buttercup petals, are inviting enough to be laid out in a design for a picture, or a simple design. I hope to show you in this book how easy it is to make useful presents for friends, or gifts for bazaars, or objects that can adorn your own home.

I have also included a number of cartoon pictures in collage, created from petals and foliage. I had never attempted collage before (except a few pictures in felt, depicting the four seasons) and I will explain later how it was that my first flower collage took shape.

Those who do not wish for disappointments would be wise to read the list of "tried favourites" in my first book, *Pressed Flower Pictures*. There they will find a detailed list of flowers and leaves that press successfully, for not all flowers do well for either colour retention or texture suitability. That book contains detailed advice on the technique of making pressed flower pictures; however, I have summarized the main points in the chapters that follow.

It is a wonderful hobby for taking one into pastures new. One makes new friends, and flowers and leaves come through the letter-box from afar from members of the "press gang"! We swap new "pressings" and share each other's joys or disappointments at the results of our latest experiments. Even holidays and walks can be sought with a view to rambles over glorious countryside, picking discriminately as new ground is explored, though I must stress that wasteful picking must be avoided as blooms must go into the pressing book fresh and "wide awake"!

Many of those who love gardening find that they can develop their natural talents in this hobby of making original designs from pressed flowers, especially as it brings garden flowers into the house during the gloomy months of winter, and provides a unique opportunity of exploiting their interest in creative activities all the year round. But also it offers much more than this, as new pictures composed at the end of a pressing season revive joys and provide souvenirs of happy summer days and holidays.

Picking and pressing is all absorbing. One takes a walk—be it in country or town—for a reason, with eyes more alert and purposeful, especially when one has a collage cartoon in mind. You will, perhaps, for the first time notice the peculiar shape of a leaf, and ask yourself whether it sparks off an idea for a new design. Is that prunus leaf just a prunus leaf? Lying there, all damp and mottled—doesn't it look like the speckly breast of a song thrush? Of course it does! Now look for its wing. A wing? Yes! A smaller leaf seems suitable and you can hardly wait to get it into the pressing book and see your "thrush" in a collage cartoon. Notice, too, and pick the summer's grasses—stalks of every kind will be most useful when picture-making begins. The hobby becomes so absorbing that one's friends also are filled with an infectious good humour to help pick. In my own fortunate case, a friend has grown a whole bed of cosmos especially for me, as my own little "plot" was bursting at the fences. When I was away, the lovely, much awaited Nelly Moser clematis came into bloom and a neighbour who had had no previous experience of pressing flowers offered to press them for me. After a breathless and rather gabbled instruction from me as I departed for the train she pressed a dozen flowers or so, most

Chippendale 'C'

I call this my Chippendale 'C' picture, because of its curves; I've used vine leaves for two curves and leaves of the bocconia poppy with their very unusual serration of leaf-edge. Gathered together in the centre is statice latifolia. The main flowers are salpiglossis. I chose out of a selection of yellows and mauves and two tones of blue. If the colour fades to cream later, the beautiful dark veins will still remain and show up well. I made great use of the vine's tendrils, which give the picture a crazed tile effect.

successfully. I had therefore fretted unnecessarily, thinking I had lost the year-long awaited clematis petals.

One knows, too, where one is always welcome, say for a certain Clematis Viticella which has such interesting and dainty navy blue and white buds and stiff wiry stalks like pencil lines. There is a garden where a beautiful bush of Honeysuckle halliana grows, of which I am given a continual supply. This variety has long buds and flowers that are very useful as "legs" in the collage cartoons. Even a visit is planned to my dentist in June, because I know that outside the surgery are some choice long-legged clovers—for pressing! A verge of grasses by a bus stop can prove rewarding—or a bank of buttercups. One very soon knows where to go for each and every petal and leaf for pressing. It is like Pelmanism, remembering where they all grow, and even though all the flowers are labelled in their pressing books, it helps if one has some sort of order. I call it "ordered chaos". The big fairy-tale book which I've had since a tiny child, holds the secrets not of fairies but of specially cherished clematis petals!

Pressing flowers in the Victorian days of 1860 was described as an art for the leisured classes. Today, in my opinion, this is far from the case. I know of busy school teachers and their pupils, nurses, house-wives, semi-invalids, and those who know how best to fill their time usefully in making gifts for bazaars with this all engaging hobby. I was once asked at a meeting how does one find time? The answer came quickly enough—"you simply turn off the telly".

Sowing, growing, picking, and pressing can hardly be described as "leisured". In fact one is hard pressed oneself! From sun up to sun down, fit the picking and pressing in between the daily chores a little at a time. When the day's work is done, find joy and peace in wandering around the garden, along the lanes, through leaf-strewn parks (in autumn), choosing one's pressings in the short time the sun is still keeping the flowers open and dew-free. No! It is not just for the so-called leisured classes, if indeed there are any left! The hobby is all enveloping in mind and in physical action. So it is up to you, the reader, to decide at what pace to "take your leisure", but I hope in any case that this book gives you plenty of ideas of how to occupy whatever time and energy you have to spare.

I

How to Press Flowers

I HAVE ALREADY DEALT at some length with the technique of picking and pressing flowers in my previous book. However, it is worth repeating the salient points and mentioning other matters which have arisen in correspondence or have been learnt from my most recent experiments; I also know from the numerous talks I have given to groups in many parts of the country the sort of problems that puzzle people, so I hope that this chapter will be of some help.

The Choice of Flowers

It is wasteful to pick every type of flower as it is not always the brightest colour which is the most suitable. Too many eager "pressers" are attracted to picking the bright blue and red flowers forgetting that blues fade very soon to a pale brown and a transparent nothing. Red becomes a chocolate brown; use it by all means but remember to make allowances for this in the colour tones of the design. Indeed, if one is to retain an over-all colour tone, it is advisable as a beginner to keep to the list in *Pressed Flower Pictures*. Here I allow for fading and therefore arrange the design in tones of beiges, deep browns, grey, chromes, silver and white. It is very satisfying to make a picture in these over-all colours for the petals have already done their fading and autumn leaves will stay brown or yellow for a number of years.

Since writing *Pressed Flower Pictures* I have tried out one or two new flowers. I always enjoy trying something new. One was the blue and yellow salpiglossis sent to me from the Isle of Man from a very keen member of the "press gang", John Kitto. These are handsome flowers with interesting dark veins running through the petals, and though the colour tends to fade the veins remain outstanding, but for how long I have not yet established.

Another flower under "test" is the fuchsia. I do not altogether "trust" its crimson petals, but its pendulous stamens and stigma are invaluable for butterfly antennae in collage pictures.

Ursinia is yet another new flower for me to press. A bed of these in several varieties makes a most gay and lively addition of colour to the garden. I grow these, like most annuals, in seed pans in the airing cupboard with the door kept open, and then prick them out later. I find that they are a little difficult to remove intact from the blotting paper after pressing, as they seem prone to fall apart, but their petal colouring—orange and dark browny-black near the centre —makes them well worth retrieving and reassembling petal by petal. They are very frail so it is essential to put only the tiniest bit of adhesive on the inside tip of the petal when fixing them to the mounting board. And, by the way, I find the petals of ursinia and gazania make effective "schools of aquarium fish" in collage designs.

I am also experimenting with red anemones, but here again each petal must be picked off and reassembled when pressed and dry.

Another new choice of flower is the tulip of which the yellow and red suffused variety, and the black Parrot tulips, seem to be the best. The latter are used in the pictures of fish, on page 61. The method is to dismantle the flower and press each petal separately.

I have also had success with pressing pussy willow. Take each fluffy young pussy before it starts to show its pollen and give it a heavy pressing. They look lovely with clematis stalks in a design with anemones, daffodils and freesias.

Colour

Yellows are fairly safe, for example buttercups will last about a year if exposed continually to the light. I have table mats of anthemis and the little "poached egg plant", limnanthes, and these have lasted best of all—ten years to date. Yellow, silver and white look particularly effective if set against a black background.

Do not expect, for example, a red or yellow rose petal to keep its colour. It will not, and this applies to most red flowers. Red does not retain its colour—it turns brown eventually. A yellow rose petal becomes beige, and so, too, does a white rose petal (the florabunda

A Very Cold Robin

The very slight curve at the end of this leaf is what I have described as a "depressed leaf"! And it made all the difference to the picture when I chose this leaf from the dozens of others picked up on a wet November Sunday afternoon.

The downward curve of the tail, beak and drooping eyelid were made by adding a small piece of absinthium leaf. Small grey artemisia leaves create the stark bareness of the winter "trees".

Iceberg is my favourite for pressing), but the latter takes on a most lovely pale brown and blends in very well with the deep brown stalks and leaves of Clematis montana and the many varieties of grey leaves, e.g. Cineraria Diamond and the silver Artemisia Absinthium, Lambrook Silver.

Notice also the many leaves whose underside is grey, namely raspberry, and the globe herbaceous thistle, echinops. The latter make very useful little "fir trees" in cartoon collage. Do grow the silver and white leaf of Senecio Greyii, as the leaves come in very handy for making "ears". Ask a friend to give you a "heel" from this plant; it strikes very quickly. The gazania leaf is a new one for me. It was sent to me through the post by an enthusiastic presser who had found its lovely slim grey underside a most welcome addition to the more usual grey-leaf plants. This leaf looks most effective on a black background and makes a very effective substitute for a daffodil leaf. It likes chalky soil and a full sunny position in the garden.

13

Daffodils

I reassembled two daffodils to make these four flowers.
The underside of gazania leaves make a most striking and admirable replacement to the daffodils' own leaves. At the base are freesia buds in place of crocus' which are too fleshy to press. Buttercups and three ursinia flowers are also included in this small picture.

The only blue flowers which retain their colour for a number of years are the dark blue delphinium and larkspur. These are picked off the stem for pressing, including all the top unopened and near-opened buds. Press six flowers to a page. Delphiniums can be pressed in their entirety—if it is a hot, dry summer—or dismantled, petal by petal, for quicker drying if the weather is inclement and then re-assembled when ready for putting into a picture.

Leaves

Do not pick green leaves, except honeysuckle (which goes a deep brown) and the earthnut or pignut which can be used also as a substitute for a delphinium and cosmos. The small side-stalk leaves of the buttercup are suitable however, and the flower, leaves and stalk can all be pressed in their entirety. I use the leaves of the meadow buttercup as hands in cartoon collage! They can be most expressive and make a figure come to life.

After the hectic summer months are over, when even one's holiday is spent in stocking up the pressing books, autumn brings a fresh choice of foliage for use both in the wall pictures and, more useful still, in the cartoon pictures as "birds"! So pick up all the fallen leaves you can, especially leaves with a pointed end. These will later become "beaks".

Autumn leaves, in their lovely frost-burnt vermilions, reds and yellows, spur one on to take walks where certain trees, e.g. the prunus leaves (as in my own town), have caught the November frost and over night have sent down a cascade of gorgeous, varying tones of red. These autumn leaves will keep their colour and will not fade any more, so one is safe to design with them. It does not matter if they are picked up in the wet, indeed it is better this way for they are more leathery and less fragile than petals and press better when slightly damp. They are improved by a rinse under the tap to wash away the grit and grime which has accumulated over the summer months. Each leaf should then be wiped with absorbent toilet paper or cloth, to take off any surplus moisture, and put between toilet tissue. The absorbent toilet paper is more economical than blotting paper, but should *only be used* for leaves and grasses.

Method of Pressing

Obviously one cannot be over precise in suggesting when a flower should be picked for pressing—I have gathered grasses by torchlight, or when waiting for a bus in a country lane, or picked up leaves as they were swept across a road by a gust of wind—nevertheless ideally blooms at least should be picked when they are neither touched by morning frost nor wet with evening dew, so I always say that midday on a fine day is best of all. If the stalk is thin enough it too should be picked (for flowers *do* grow on stalks and people often forget it when making designs), and the whole thing should be placed as soon as possible between two sheets of blotting paper and then put immediately between the pages of a book, though not one of shiny "art" paper as this is not sufficiently absorbent. Put a paper tag in the page naming the flower, as this is a great help as a sort of index to the flowers and leaves that are available for inclusion in a pressed flower design in the autumn. When one page has been sufficiently filled move to about five or six pages further on and so on through the book, labelling as you go. Then put a brick or heavy weight on the book and *leave undisturbed* for at least four weeks. It is this consistent heavy weight which makes or mars a successful pressing and, most important of all, *do not look* at your flower or leaf pressing in the book *at all* in the first important four weeks.

For this hobby all one needs is patience, enthusiasm, determination and a methodical mind. Very little expenditure is involved, with the exception of buying blotting paper which can be costly if one is wasteful. About February I go through the now near-empty pressing books and take out and dry off the old blotting paper and pressing books ready for the new pressing season again.

Children especially ask me whether they cannot use a substitute for blotting paper as they don't have enough pocket money to buy very much. I am a little reluctant to advise the use of absorbent toilet papers, hankies and napkins because some have a very fine wrinkled line pattern in the paper and this would be transferred on to a petal's fine texture. However, some economy can be made by pressing leaves only between absorbent toilet papers, as I have suggested earlier. Also remember that although the outlay for the first year's blotting paper

Yellow freesias being taken off their stem and placed between blotting paper in a book of the absorbent, non-shiny type of paper. Notice the all-important labelling to each page of pressings.

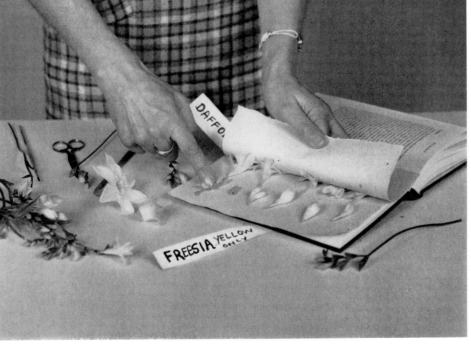

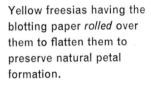

Yellow freesias having the blotting paper *rolled* over them to flatten them to preserve natural petal formation.

Small daffodils with orange trumpets being dismantled for pressing. The trumpet is split down the middle as a complete flower is too fleshy to press successfully as a whole.

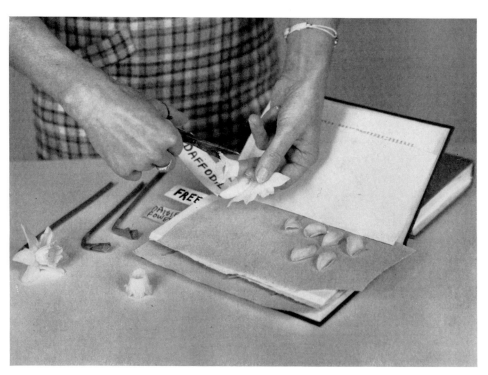

A busy scene of "pressings" in December. Red anemone petals are being dismantled because this flower has a "complicated corolla". On the right are 4-week-old pressed anemone petals. In the foreground are last February's tulip petals and stamens, and on the left are daffodil trumpets.

may prove costly, it can be used for several years if it is dried and treated with care. And I have one suggestion: I have been known to collect up all the less crumpled and almost unused paper napkins after a meal out at a restaurant or hotel—to the raised eyebrows of the waiters, but with the helpful encouragement from pressed flower enthusiasts who know how useful these absorbent napkins are for pressing autumn leaves!

Some people take their flowers out of the pressing books and put them in cellophane packets after so many weeks, to make room for more, but I do not recommend this. Petals, though looking well pressed and dry, can, if they are left for months out of their blotting paper book "beds", begin to absorb the moisture in the air, and with changes of temperature, warmth and humidity the petals can react and begin to crinkle and, once really dried out, will never be completely smooth again. There is nothing sadder than a wrinkled, badly pressed flower. It must be perfect. Pressing flowers is rather like ironing a linen pillow-case. If linen is ironed too dry, it will never become really smooth. It is the same with petals. Petals contain a certain amount of natural moisture and the pressure of a brick hastens the drying process, at the same time making the petal completely smooth. It will remain smooth like this as long as it is away from extremes of temperature, or humidity. This is assured by placing glass on the picture (or a sheet of adhesive, paper-thin, transparent plastic material for smaller articles, e.g. matchboxes, calendars, etc.) and seeing that a picture is backed with hardboard and the glass sealed round with adhesive tape. It is also important that the pressing books are kept in a well-aired, dry room.

You will gather from what I have written so far that I am a firm believer in "books and bricks" as the ideal pressers. Books are quicker to use when the season is in full spate. One cannot hope to possess enough screw-presses to do all one's flowers at once so each batch would have to be turned out to make room for the next. A screw-press applies too much pressure to the more delicate flowers and squashes them to a horrid mess of unrecognizable petals. Nevertheless I fully accept that there are advantages in using a proper press for flowers with hard centres, for instance anthemis and pussy willow. In such a

Shown here are flowers and leaves being pressed under bricks. The press on the right was especially made for me by my engineer cousin and is used only for pressing flowers with hard centres. The pieces of hardboard on the right go between each square of blotting paper and pressings.

case I place them in a flower press and screw down fairly firmly. A few hours later the screw can be turned a little more and perhaps again the following morning. On the second day, I release the pressure and very carefully substitute a fresh piece of blotting paper as these bulkier flowers contain a fair amount of moisture and if allowed to remain in damp blotting paper will go mouldy. This must be done quickly, with as little disturbance as possible. I leave them for another day or two, then remove them carefully into fresh blotting paper and put them in the normal pressing books, and then weight the pressing with two bricks for about a week, after which I remove one brick to allow the book to "breathe", otherwise mould may develop. You can see how this does not contrast very well with the easier, but admittedly less hasty, method of using books throughout the pressing and drying out process, when flowers, stalks and leaves can be left indefinitely without coming to any harm. I have had leaves and flowers still pressed in books for three years that are still in good condition and completely smooth. It is a mistake to try to get quick results.

20

Pressing of some petals separately

It is only with honeysuckle, rudbeckia, clematis, pussy willow, tulip, anemone, daffodil, freesia, gazania, rose (and if a wet summer, delphinium) that the petals are pulled off the corolla and pressed petal by petal in books, and then reassembled exactly as they grew, when dried and pressed. When pressing the small yellow Welsh poppy (which dries out a lovely melon colour), Icelandic poppy, tulip and anemone only, the stigma is nipped out first. Leave the poppies' stamens intact. These little Welsh poppies' circular mass of stamens make very useful "middles" for all sorts of flowers, e.g. clematis and rose. Poppies are prolific self-sowers and pop up all over my little plot and when they are in seed I spend a rare moment sitting still in my deckchair watching some field mice run up the frail stems to raid the seed pods.

Polyanthus & primula are all cut --- off at the back of their petals

For primula (puce-coloured variety) and polyanthus (dark red) nip their heads off just behind the petals, leaving the calyx piece as illustrated in the margin.

For pressing tulips, pick off each petal and place two or three to a page. Be brave! Do not be put off by their somewhat cup-shaped petal. Use a rolling movement with the blotting paper and a few pages of the book over the petals—they will press out beautifully—those which split can be used for either butterfly wings or fishes' tails. They will resemble satin after six weeks' of pressing. The black Parrot tulips are particularly stunning with their raggly, uneven-edged petals and can be used in the collage pictures, for instance as a fish, or the long hair of a Victorian miss!

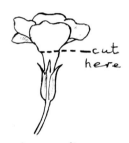

--- cut here

when putting them into the books to press

Pluck honeysuckle petals from their knobbly centre and distribute them on a page and, when pressed and dry, reassemble as they once grew. Little buds at the top, and more open buds next and then the fuller open flower, ensuring the standard (big top) petal is uppermost.

Another flower which is too bulky to press as a whole is the gazania. Because its corolla is impossibly thick to press, and because its petals curl up when carried into the shade, take the pressing book and blotting paper into the garden to this plant. Pull off each gay yellow petal with its little black full-stop marking on its "throat", and place in the

A pond primula after it has been cut off as shown above as dotted line.

pressing book immediately. Also pick the lovely dark green pencil-slim leaves, mentioned earlier. I managed to continue picking these leaves right up until December by bringing a few plants inside in pots.

Finally a word of advice about curves which are often sadly lacking in beginners' first pictures. It is very well worth while picking and pressing as many clematis, clover, daisy and primrose stalks as you have room for and ensuring that some are pressed in a curve as these are essential to the designs of many pictures.

Mock-up flowers from loose petals

If some of your flowers, as whole flowers, have not turned out a success, do not throw them away. Save the petals if the centre corolla has disintegrated and with, say, a delphinium, an ursinia or an anthemis make up your own do-it-yourself "flower". Make use of astrantia for a centre (I use these as wheels or hats in the cartoon collage designs) and place the odd, loose petals around it.

Sometimes it is the other way round, for instance the petals of a Welsh poppy have pressed poorly, but yet its centre whorl of stamens is perfect. Use this stamen, then, as a centre piece to dark blue delphinium petals and make it into a "mock" periwinkle-type flower. Never throw away loose petals. You will be surprised at the number of uses a single petal can be put to, especially in the cartoon pictures.

Single petals are especially useful in collage pictures. A freesia petal can make a duck's beak, an orange ursinia petal can become a fish in a school of tiny fishes. In the same way as in unsuccessful flower pressings, leaves, mainly the autumn brown ones, are actually welcomed by me when badly pressed! These misshapened leaves give one ideas for new designs. One might look like part of a bird, a person's face, or a hat. There is no need to cut it. Leave it as it is and just add the necessary parts to make it what it almost resembles. It's very exciting and one finds oneself smiling to oneself as the leaf suddenly stirs one's imagination and becomes a little person, or a furry animal, or what you will.

The skill (as well as the fun) is, I think, in not cutting a leaf or petal, but using it as it is. That is the challenge.

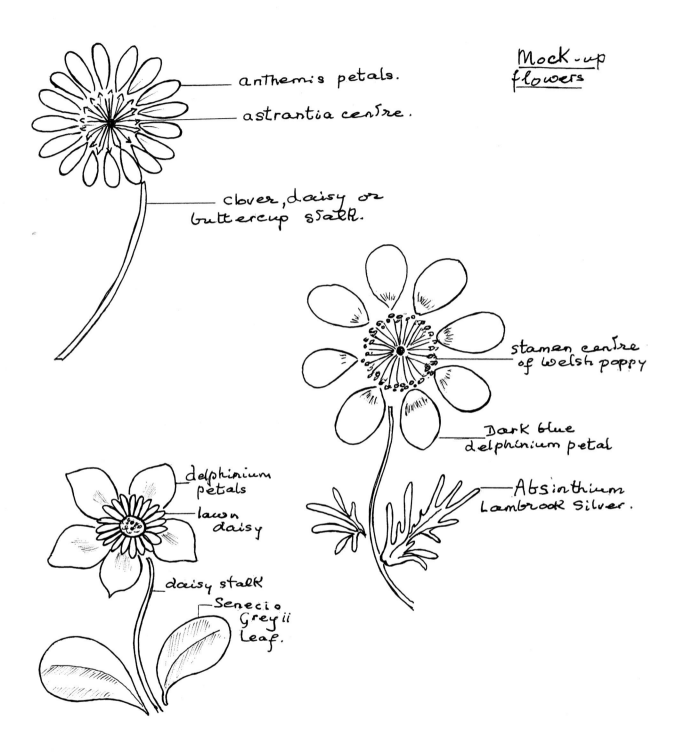

anthemis petals.

astrantia centre.

Mock-up
flowers

clover, daisy or
buttercup stalk.

stamen centre
of welsh poppy

Dark blue
delphinium petal

Absinthium
Lambrook Silver.

delphinium
petals

lawn
daisy

daisy stalk

Senecio
Greyii
Leaf.

stamens from fuchsia

Orange coloured
Ursinia petals

— deeper orange bud
of montbretia.

Meadow buttercup
leaves
& stem.

Once a gaillardia — but badly
pressed it has become
an Aidralliag!
using the meadow
buttercup's stalks
& buds.

Sticking down pressed flowers

I use a not-too-sticky glue which has a latex or rubberized solution base and one which remains usable after it has been squeezed out of its tube for as long as twenty minutes. This is a great advantage. Most stationers or drug stores can produce one of these latex solutions which, if one sticks a flower on wrongly, can be easily removed by rubbing off—with a clean finger. No trace will remain to mar the design.

Some people use tweezers for handling delicate petals, but I prefer an ordinary paint brush for lifting and moving them about the design. Use the fluffy end for moving petals and then turn the brush round to use the tip of the wooden handle, dip it into the adhesive and apply it to the flower, leaf or stem. Only put the "sticky" on the centre of the corolla if a whole flower is being used. If you're sticking single petals put the tiniest possible amount on the inside edge tip of the petal. Don't worry if the other end of the petal flaps about, as it is only temporary until the glass is placed over the design.

Sticking grasses seems to send would-be pressers into unnecessary panic! There is no need to smother all the stem in adhesive. Simply stroke the back of the grass with the handle end of the brush with "sticky" and as long as it catches just one or two parts of the stem or seed head this is sufficient to hold it all down.

As a general guide for applying the latex solution—
note the diagrams here and on the following page, in
which the thick lines indicate where the adhesive
should be applied, very sparingly.

DO'S AND DON'TS

1. Do get in a good supply of blotting paper and absorbent type toilet paper for the start of the pressing season, i.e. April for primrose stalks, earthnut or pignut leaves, daffodil petals and trumpets, and tulips.

2. Do dry off last year's blotting papers and re-use.

3. Do press the flowers in a book which has absorbent-type pages. *Not* in a book which is printed on shiny paper.

4. Do keep a special book for stalks. An old wallpaper pattern book is ideal.

5. Don't pick every flower you see. Be discriminate. Aim for the yellow flowers with a simple corolla, not too lumpy.

6. Don't pick blue or mauve flowers with the exception of delphinium and larkspur and the puce-coloured pond primula.

7. Do pick on a dry, sunny day.

8. Don't, as a general rule, pick green leaves.

9. Do pick leaves which are green on top but grey or silver on the underside, i.e. raspberry, echinops, gazania and wolf's-bane.

10. Don't press too heavily—nor too lightly. Allow the book and pressings to "breathe" occasionally to avoid mildew.

11. Do see that some stalks are pressed in a curve.

12. Do see that autumn leaves *only* are damp when put to the press, and change their absorbent tissue or toilet paper at the end of a week and replace with dry tissue.

13. Do see the pressing books are kept in a well-aired room.

14. Don't overcrowd the design. Let every leaf and petal stand out.

15. Do use a paint brush, fluffy end, to move the pressed flowers about on the designing board.

16. Do arrange the entire design of the pressed flower, first, and *then* stick all down together.

17. Don't use too much glue when sticking down a design. Put the adhesive only on the corolla and on the inner tip of a single petal. Never all over it (*see* diagrams on pages 25–6).

18. Do see your finger is really clean before rubbing off excess latex adhesive on the board!

19. Do place a piece of blotting paper on top of the design and then a sheet of glass on top of that if you are interrupted while making your picture and have to leave it, to ensure the dryness is preserved.

20. Do paint the *stalks only* of Clematis montana with a mild antiseptic lotion to ensure no mildew over the years.

21. Do *not* mount your pressed flower picture as the mount will prevent the glass pressing on the flowers and thus stopping them curling.

22. Do see that the design is framed and covered in glass and that the flowers are pressed well up to the glass.

Autumn Leaves
(October's offerings)

Many varieties of autumn leaves encircle the dark stem of Clematis montana. Allow some of the leaves to overlay the stem to break up the too obvious line of the stem. The flowers are Hagley Hybrid clematis, ground elder and Anthemis Cupaniana. Note serration of the Turkey oak leaves and the sprays of small, mauve-grey acaena leaves.

Pamela McDowall 1970.

23. Do have the picture backed in hardboard to ensure adequate pressure.

24. Do remember when arranging a design that FLOWERS GROW FROM STALKS!

25. Do aim to grow, try out and test for suitability a few new flowers and leaves each year.

26. Don't forget grasses and especially *do* grow the ornamental grasses from those shown in seed catalogues.

27. And don't, whatever you do, give a huge sigh of relief (or cough!) at your newly designed, but as yet unstuck, picture—unless you want to spend another hour picking up and retrieving your blown away pressed flowers! This also goes as a warning against draughts and the slamming of doors!

Flanders Poppies

I do not know how these lovely Flanders poppies came to grow in my little plot but they were a most welcome surprise and as each flower opened it was carefully taken to the pressing books. Having seen that its colour retained fairly well I have since ordered a packet of seed to be sure of further reliable stocks. In place of the poppy's stigma (which must be nipped out before pressing) and this poppy's stamens (which disintegrated) I placed a white astrantia in the centre. Do not use the stem of the poppy, it is too hard. Use any curved stalk. I've used my favourite stem of Clematis montana and also Clematis Viticella which has so fine a stem it is like a line drawn with a pen. I particularly like Clematis Viticella's little navy blue and white striped buds. which have been added to the montana stems.

2

Designing Pressed Flower Pictures

I AM OFTEN ASKED "How do you start on a design? Do you draw it out first?" The answer is a very definite "No". For the simple reason one cannot draw out a picture if one does not have the exact knowledge of what has pressed well over the summer months, in the pressing books. It isn't until I have had a good browse through the books and suddenly come across, say, a particularly good pressing that I am inspired to use that special flower, or even a suitably curved stalk, as the starting point and so build around it.

In *Pressed Flower Pictures* I described the curves of stalks as the limbs of a line of chorus girls. It is the same with plants. Without the gracefulness of curved stalks, flowers would look like stiff little marionettes. For even when a plant's centre stem is growing upright the leaves have a curve somewhere. So, keep all this natural growth of curves in your arrangement.

Some pressed flower pictures produced by beginners can only be described as spotted and jerky, stiff and over-smothered. Think of a fan, be it upright or sideways. Make its base compact and "busy", and use an interesting leaf or a dominant flower as a central piece from which the rest of the design can spring. After you are satisfied with the base, branch out—with confidence—with curved stalks at the side with, say, grasses, clovers, daisies, and use primrose stalks (not the flower) with another flower head as a substitute. Only the centre stalks in the design need then be straight. Leaves play a big part in softening up a picture and I also use a favourite grass such as barren brome or trembling grass. I dismantle barren brome after pressing and use each little bewhiskered prawn-like frond to taper off the corners of the design.

Which inspires you first— the flower or the stalk? Sometimes I find the stalk is the easiest. If so, begin like this:

1. You may have to nip off pieces from several stems to make the exact curve but what remains can be used another time.

2. Now add the main flower, for example clematis with anthemis either side. Nip out part of the now unwanted parts of the stalk from underneath the flowers so as to avoid any undue lumpiness.

3. At this stage add in a few curved side stems. Try and keep each flower and leaf quite separate from the next.

Grasses, to my eye, are like arms and hands reaching out—expressing their feelings, as indeed they do as they react in wind, rain and sun. They are always graceful—curving and bending like ice-skaters, sheer poetry in line—when placed in the correct position in a picture design.

Then there's the question of colouring. Let me make it quite plain that I do not colour pressed flowers, with the exception of white daisies, cow parsley, ground elder and the little "whirls" of white clover, which I paint with white poster paint. The flowers you press are not chosen for their brightness but more for the shape of the petal and the serration of a leaf, and it is more important to know what colour they will turn into after three or four weeks of pressing and in the years to come than to take any notice of their colour when they are picked.

I advise designing the picture in a balanced tone of greys, beige, fawns, yellows, dark brown and white. Two ideal yellow flowers are the herbaceous daisy anthemis and limnanthes. These both show up well on a black background and retain their colour for some years. Remember that all pictures should be hung on a north wall, away from strong direct sunlight.

Starting a design

When confronted with the plain mounting cardboard do you "shy like a pit pony"? Do you deliberate before it? Hesitant, yet longing to begin, but with no clear idea as to where to start or even what shape the design will take? Don't worry! Churchill felt just the same with his first attempts at oils and started with a cloud—which he described as resembling a bean, until an artist came up and took the brush out of his hand and smothered the canvas in bold strokes. And look what masterpieces he produced later—it was only with practice and determination that this was attained.

First, have a good look through the pressing book. A particularly eye-catching flower which has pressed well can start you off. Take it out and place it beside your board, still keeping it in between its blotting papers, for you do not know how long it will be before you find the rest of your pressed materials nor do you know if you are going to be called away to some mundane household chore!

4. For the final stages add some honeysuckle to break up the too defined curved line. Montbretia bud fronds, mimosa and heuchera make nice flower bed curves. Repeat on the other side to make the colour or "bobbly" design balance. Leave them as they are on the board and lift up (with the fluffy end of the brush) the main stalk line, keeping it still in place but rubbing a bit of glue underneath the stems. Pat down with the fingers. Now do the same with the main flower's petals. Do not disturb the formation, just lift the inner tip of the petal, and put a tiny bit of "sticky" on and press down. Stick all the flowers in exactly the same way.

32

Autumn Gold

An autumn leaf toned design—browns, orange and golds of montbretia, anthemis, freesia and honeysuckle predominate. The grey underside of raspberry leaves and white of Anthemis Cupaniana make a welcome contrast to the sombre browns of prunus, Clematis montana and one blackberry leaf. "Bobbles" of mimosa show up well on Clematis montana leaves.

Iceberg

This picture is dominated by the two large "flowers" which are
created from the petals of my favourite white rose, floribunda
Iceberg, and, as a centrepiece, the stamen of Welsh poppies. These
are enclosed within an almost closed letter C, reversed, which is
made from the stem of a Clematis montana. As the pattern of flowers
and leaves are added the stem is cut away so as to make the whole
as smooth as possible when it is covered with glass.

The main tones are yellows, chromes, golds, browns, greys and some
very dark, almost black leaves. The flowers include yellow freesias,
honeysuckle, yellow mimulus and anthemis and white Anthemis
Cupaniana (the petals of which have been touched with white poster
paint to retain their colour) and mimosa which turns to a deep
orange over the years. The leaves are the soft beige underside of
raspberry leaves, some grey senecio and, in contrast, some ash
leaves which were picked when they were greeny-red but have
turned almost black and are used here to terminate the sprigs of
mimosa.

Pamela McDowall 1959

Tulip Flowers

This is one of my biggest pictures. The yellow tulip petals are all pressed singly and surround a gaillardia flower. Between each petal are the tulip's stamens. The paleness of the tulip petals needed the fiery red and yellow dominance of the gaillardia—one of the few "reds" that I press. These are placed as centrepieces to bring out the design and give it more body. On the outer edge of the tulip, and between each, are ginkgo leaves. The small, thin-stemmed fronds of the cherry prunus were picked when this tree started to grow new crimson-coloured growth of young shoots. The leaves dry out almost black when pressed.

Dispersed between the fronds, as if growing from this tree, are yellow freesias, and also two brown flowers (once red) of mimulus. A few raspberry leaves help to relieve the rather austere dark prunus. Mimosa fills the centre base, and honeysuckle is growing and going where it feels inclined.

July's Offerings

A dark background is ideal for showing up flowers of yellows and white, and the grey or white underside of leaves, providing the picture is not too big. My preferred limit is $24\frac{1}{2}'' \times 21''$.

This is the only time when the ground elder, with its dainty umbels of florets, comes into its own. These, like the cow parsley, are painted white. So too is the white Anthemis Cupaniana, and the little "whorl" in the clover's head picked out in white paint. The other "whites" in the picture are the underside leaves of Senecio Greyii. Included in the daisy group is my favourite Anthemis tinctoria, "Grallagh Gold", and in the cluster on the right of the design are four miniature narcissi, "Baby Moon", which were small enough to press in their entirety.

Cosmos in Collage

I started the design, seeing and knowing I had a good selection of lovely, well pressed cosmos flowers, grown for me by a friend whose garden contained a moister soil than my own. The design was started with one, then two big, dominant cosmos and then the base. The vase is in collage of wool material, of the same colour tones as the cosmos, taken from one of my dresses. The left-hand side of the vase has (to give it a more definite outline) one single grass stem, curved, alongside it. This acts like a pencil line. The right-hand side of the vase has been "shaded" with petals of cosmos. In this picture I laid the flowers on first and the stalks on afterwards. The outer edge of the bouquet has "fillers-in" of the dainty little Heuchera sanguinea, and the deep blue of larkspur, buds and all. The stem may be any stalk from, say, primrose, buttercup or Clematis montana. The larkspur flowers were bought at a florist's and each flower pressed separately and then reassembled and stuck down exactly as it once grew. I've used the silver leaves of Artemisia Absinthium Lambrook Silver as this is similar, but prettier, than the cosmos's own foliage. Curving gracefully over the sides of the vase are the silver undersides of four gazania leaves, and also two dark brown Clematis montana leaves to break up the pastel tones.

Simplicity

A very delicate, pastel toned design. The stems of Clematis montana and the flowerless honeysuckle with its spotted leaves make it clear and defined. Even when the mauve primula flowers fall back to brown this will not detract from the overall tones of the beige rose petals (Iceberg), with centres of rock rose and a honeysuckle which is lovely to use and well worth the effort to reassemble when pressed.

Let us presume you've found some well pressed rose petals, clematis, dark blue delphinium flowers or cosmos. Move all these books near your board, or take the flowers out in their blotting paper, with their labels, and place near you.

Here a design is fan shaped, on its side.

Backgrounds

Some people prefer a background of material such as shantung, silk or velvet, but I prefer mounting board. This is water-colour board and can be bought at any art shop in white and cream, or black. For big pictures I use the cream side, but for covering matchboxes, ordinary white card or thin cardboard is quite suitable. It is no use choosing a gold-fawn background for a design which includes ferns, as in a few months the ferns will turn to gold and so "fall back" into the same tone as the background and be "lost".

The yellow pansy (use only the yellow and black), buttercups, anthemis (of which there are three yellow toned varieties) and limnanthes, also white daisy and the many grey-silver leaves, look lovely on table mats with black backgrounds. Grey and white leaves and flowers respond well on a crimson blotting paper background. This material adapts itself well, stuck on with a very little latex-type adhesive to the mounting board.

Framing pictures

It is *essential* that the flowers are well pressed up against the glass. The pictures should *never* be mounted. Ask the picture framer to back the picture with hardboard, as this applies the necessary pressure to the picture, and thereby keeps the petals flat. Remember if there is just one over-lumpy flower centre, or stalk, this prevents the rest of the flowers from getting the essential, continued pressing.

and here a centre fan-like design.

Before beginning a design it is advisable to order your frame and glass after deciding on the size of the mounting board. But even if the picture frame is not ready when you start the design it is useful to have a spare piece of picture glass which you can place over your mounting board and flowers to preserve them from damp and at the same time keep them flat while waiting for the frame to arrive.

41

When the frame is made and the design finished, tack the picture into the frame with temporary tacks or seal round with adhesive tape just to keep the picture intact for the journey to the picture framer's shop. Allow for wind and rain. Wrap it all up in a plastic bag or a sack made from an old blanket. This latter method is ideal if the pictures are big (or if one travels around a lot with them as I do) for it protects the edges from hard knocks. And knocks there can be if one is caught on a windy day carrying a large picture and is blown along, somewhat out of control, like a ship in full sail in a crowded harbour!

Red Anemone

A rare occasion when I use red in a design, but knowing these red anemone petals will turn brown and be a tone lighter than the dark Clematis montana leaves and stems, they are quite suitable to use. Ground elder (painted white) is placed on each anemone's centre and interspersed up the centre stem. The base is finished off neatly with mimosa and the dainty ornamental grass, briza minor.

3

Cartoon Pictures in Collage

Each leaf segment can be used for a left or right hand.
Cineraria Diamond.

IT WAS QUITE BY ACCIDENT that I nearly tripped over my first little collage cartoon figure. It was lying on the petal-strewn floor at my foot. I had just finished the last big flower picture for an exhibition and was glad to stretch an aching back from the kneeling position in which I work at my pictures. Here all the pressing books are within an arm's stretch beside me on the floor. As I surveyed the inglorious, chaotic state of the floor, there, amongst the loose, straying petals (not yet tidied away into their specially labelled pressing books) was a solitary clover head. Lying almost on top of it was a single Senecio Greyii leaf. To me it looked like a very shy little face peeping out at me from behind a "fan". In a second I knelt down to find the "face", some "arms" and "legs" and a "skirt". Bits of Clematis montana's "twiggle" (next year's frond shoots) at once became the lady's high-heeled shoes and legs (this was before discovering that honeysuckle buds were more effective). A daffodil trumpet became her mini-skirt and in less than five minutes the first little "I'm shy" cartoon collage in nature's own foliage was made. So, out of what can only be described as "ordered chaos", came an entirely new sort of pressed flower picture—the collage cartoon, which has been of absorbing interest and great entertainment value to me ever since. It was a revelation, indeed.

As the summer went by and I was stocking up with pressed flowers, it seemed that the more disordered the floor became the quicker new figures were made. I have found that making these little petalled-people is easier than drawing. Figure drawing has never come easily to me, but here it seemed that by simply pushing a honeysuckle bud "leg" this way or that (with a dry paint brush) one could make a figure either stand up or fall down—in a second! There is no need to

43

"I'm Shy"

My very first cartoon. Because I noticed one clover head peeping out from behind a Senecio Greyii leaf the first little cartoon was "born". All the other cartoons followed almost as easily and as accidentally as this one.

J'm shy

draw anything. The shapes of "heads, bodies or legs" are ready made for you if you choose from the list on pages 71–6. Use the spring and summer for gathering flower and grass material for your flower pictures, and the autumn for the cartoon collage in leaves, for there is great fun to be had looking for "shapes" in autumn leaves, particularly the various cherry prunus leaves which fill the streets where I live. I intend one day to make a crocodile using the leaves of Turkey oak for its teeth!

By November the roads and lanes as well as my garden were smothered in wind-blown autumn leaves, and especially inviting were the ones touched by the first frost. I had often regretted the hurried, and sometimes careless, pressing of these leaves, but imagine the revelation and inspiration which took hold when, as the pages of the large wallpaper patterned books (with absorbent toilet paper between the pages) were flicked over, a bent leaf had, in its inadvertent careless

Spinsters are Unclaimed Treasures.

Spinsters Are Unclaimed Treasures

The little lady on the right shows confidence, not only with her reassuring hand-patting but with her perky hat "feather"—a stark, upright honeysuckle flower. While the bigger spinster's character is shown in the two drooping lines of her hat embellishment!
Both the ladies wear shoes of "real" laburnum and broom "leather" respectively. Do you like her striped navy blue and grey handbag? It was a Clematis Jackmannii bud until I bit it in half to "cut it down to size"!

pressing, become—a bird! To my eyes, the scarlet prunus leaves were robins! The mottled leaves of prunus, picked up when very damp, were safe to use after only five days of pressing. They were taken out as—song thrushes, with lovely speckled chests!

No scissors are needed. Just an occasional stalk nipped off with a sharp thumb nail is all that is used throughout the entire series of the collage pictures, with the exception of a silvery honesty seed case cut to resemble a small air bubble or a fish's eye. Only once was I nearly defeated— the picture of the "Spinsters", one little lady's handbag of a Clematis Jackmannii bud would have been too big had I not bitten it in half!

Now that my eyes were open to the idea I found that robins, blackbirds and thrushes lay in their thousands in the gutters. All they needed was a sponge down to clean off the summer's grime and grit. That year I saw that they were made into realistic robins before the pressing book was closed! In other words, the leaf was folded over a

45

A small autumn cherry prunus becomes a little bird by simply folding over a small quarter of one side of the leaf. Add a couple of petals from any daisy or gaillardia or cotton-grass and you have given him a fine tail. His tiny feet can be buttercup leaves providing they are shaped into a curve to give them "clinging" power.

And a wing? Well, add another, smaller leaf, tuck it under the folded back leaf.

An autumn birch leaf would be suitable for his wing.

quarter. Enough to give it a "fine chest" and pointed beak. The "beak" is just the continuation of the leaf's pointed end. One leaf I noticed in the street looked depressed! A depressed leaf? Oh! come now! But yes, the pointed end of the leaf turned down, just a tiny bit. Enough for me to see a "depressed, cold robin". So now leaves are sometimes folded for birds' bodies and some are left purposely unfolded as they go into the book to be pressed. These unfolded, open leaves are for "wings". When the leaves are dry enough, in about a week, simply tuck the open, smaller leaf under the fold of the other folded leaf and at once you have your "bird on the wing"! This leaf, flower and grass collage is fascinating. A leaf has for me a double meaning, so to speak. It is not just a leaf. It is a member of my "tiny people's world". Grasses suddenly become poplar trees. The smallest leaves of the herbaceous globe thistle, echinops, become fir trees. Honeysuckle buds are a "must". It is wise to get in a good stock of these in summer to give your figures "life" on which to skip along! The barren brome grass placed at the appropriate angle indicates speed, depending on which way it is slanted. A single stem of grass is used for the horizons and slopes.

One day I was showing my publisher my collection of collage cartoons when he noticed that there were no male figures among them.

"Could you, for example, make a soldier out of leaves and petals?" he asked.

"Perhaps," I replied, "if I had some bigger autumn leaves. Have you any?"

"Have we not! How many do you want? I can give you two tons," he remarked gaily.

Thus I managed to enthuse all six foot two of him into searching out and picking up for pressing (though it rained all that weekend) some splendid horse chestnut and sweet chestnut leaves. These he pressed in a weekly supplement between absorbent kitchen paper and handed to me a week later. These leaves were a very welcome addition to my small leaf collection. He had even remembered my request to "Press a few leaves badly—at an angle, or crooked, you never know, it's the few odd-shaped leaves which may start me off on an idea." And sure enough it did! But not a soldier as the leaves eventually

46

Perhaps the easiest of all to make is a sailing ship using three autumn prunus leaves. Each leaf is folded evenly over at the time of pressing in the books. For mast and rigging use the stems of grasses. "Waves" are made with petals of delphinium. Don't forget a sea gull if you have two loose white daisy petals to spare. A buttercup bud makes a sea gull's head, and a piece of dark stalk or leaf represents its body. Paint the two daisy petal "wings" with white poster paint.

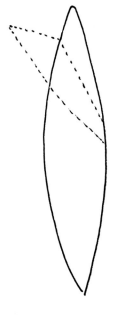

This could be a willow or any slim, pointed leaf. Bend it over and you've nearly made a penguin!

Add a leaf on either side for wings, and an orange daffodil trumpet split up to make two feet.

A song thrush can be made in a similar way, using a prunus leaf which should be longer and thinner.
Find one that has been lying on wet grass or in the gutter where it has become mottled and spotted. This gives the "thrush" a nice spotted chest.

This is a laburnum, or broom flower. For shoes.

Add two long buds of the honeysuckle halleana variety and you have the "legs" for the shoes.

A daffodil trumpet. Pressed in the winter months (bought from florists) or in spring from your garden. When cut in half, each trumpet makes two mini-skirts, for the younger people. For the not-so-young, the larger daffodil trumpet is more suitable.

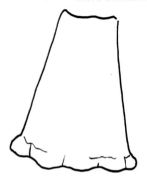

became a cartoon I call "Farmer Barley Corn", illustrated on page 70.

Keep the picture very simple and uncluttered. This advice cannot be emphasized too much. Even in pen and ink cartoons the maxim is always to use as few lines as possible. "Expression" is given to the figure with the fingers and eyes. Buttercup leaves are ideal for hands, and for animals' paws or a gloved hand use Cineraria Diamond. This is grey on top and white on the underside. Each section of the leaf has a ready-made right or left "thumb".

A cartoon is nothing without a really good eye, and it *makes* the picture. I generally draw the eyes on white paper and stick them on. But I must be truthful—I have given one of the fish a silver honesty seed case cut down to a small circle. Their seeds could make a nice pupil, but are too lumpy to use and a pressed flower picture must be absolutely flat so that the individual leaves cannot curl under the glass.

It is an advantage to leave the cartoon (or a flower picture) unstuck for a few days, but under glass. This allows time for rearrangement and a change of mind to the angle of a "leg" or "arm". Seeing it at intervals throughout the day helps one to see one's mistakes.

Once these foliage cartoons had been started, a walk was never taken without returning with pockets stuffed with leaves. Clovers on the roadside were "heads". Later, in the following year, a welcome change of hairstyle for my little people (admittedly a little unruly and wind-swept!) came in a gift of a seed head from Austria of Anemone Pulsatilla (Pasque flower) and then from the yellow clematis seed head, tangutica. It is a speaking likeness of the bouffant hair styles caught in the wind or, when picked early in seed, is more compact and so (depending on how the seed heads were pressed) becomes the bobbed hair style. Some clematis seed heads are more raggle-taggly than others and one never knows really until one opens the pressing books which way the "wind" has blown! A few stray "moulting" seed heads made Billy Goat's beard!

So in the middle of preparing for an Exhibition of pressed flower pictures, with the house and garden crying out for attention, the muddle of the flower-room floor could not be tidied up. If it had, many of the pictures you are about to see of the petalled "people" might have been lost—for ever.

48

"Be My Doll, Mop-Top"

The obvious choice for a hippie's hair style was Clematis tangutica. The Dolly girl's petalled legs were made from a gerbera daisy, bought while waiting for a train at a London station. Its red petals seemed more shapely than the more usual choice of a honeysuckle bud, however I would not use this daisy again as it doesn't retain its colour, but as it is a nice slim petal it makes an ideal "stocking" for it will turn brown. One of her shoes is a small laburnum. It took me about half an hour to get the correct angle and stance of these!
Her boy friend is wearing his "flower power" medallion—one mimosa bobble!

ME
SHOPPING!

PMED. 1969

Me Shopping !

Here expression is conveyed by the hand and fingers, made from buttercup leaves.
No face is necessary, the angle of the annual chrysanthemum flower (and badly
pressed too!) actually helps to put the cheeky humour in this cartoon. Speed is shown
by the grass "scarf", and a use is found for the stray centre stamens of Welsh poppy
by giving the shopping trolley its little wheels.

THE GOSSIPS.

PweD. 1965

The Gossips

The usual focal point for expression is made by the eyes, but as these are not visible, the humour must depend on the expressive hands and contrasting shape of the legs
The underside of a large and small whitebeam leaf give the "well endowed" lady her coat.
A cherry prunus leaf, pressed in August, with pussy willow collar, makes a nice ensemble for Mrs. Thin Lady. Both have helichrysum hats.

P.McD. 22.8.70   "Are we the same?"

"Are We the Same?"

This picture was created only because a friend expressed a wish to look through my
pressing books. As the pages were flipped over, ideas tumbled out from both of us.
A small sweet chestnut leaf and a folded-over prunus leaf caused the friend to call
out—"Look! look—there's a hedgehog!" Hilariously, there and then, we feverishly
created our hedgehog (the one on the right of the picture). It was fun to see that
someone else too had so quickly caught the idea of seeing leaf shapes as objects.
It became a game!
The hedgehog on the left didn't get made until, quite by chance, and to my great
delight, a family arrived at the front door with a single pine needle found on an
Ashdown Forest ramble.
"Would this do for a hedgehog?" they asked.
It would indeed!
Picture making becomes infectious—friends and neighbours turn up with their most
welcome and unexpected "finds"—and so the idea grows.

"Dignity & Impudence"

Pamela McDowall 7.8.70

"Dignity and Impudence"

When handling the various opening stages of the honeysuckle flower I had often
thought how some of the almost fully open flowers resembled a carthorse's and
saluki dog's fluffy feet. It was on my seeing an overblown, disintegrated Clematis
tangutica seedhead that my fingers started to create a tiny Yorkshire terrier from the
silky hair-like seed fronds. The small dog needed a contrasting companion—and the
saluki seemed to be the answer, and was very easy to make as every piece of
honeysuckle came into use to make up the entire dog. Barren brome grass made an
expressive tail. The ornamental grass, briza minor, became trees together with fennel,
picked on a Cornish bankside. The upright barley whiskers show us that the little
terrier is the "Dignity" and is "standing his ground"!

53

"Mrs. Buttercup and Baby"

A sense of movement is given here by the slanting grasses (poplar trees!). Notice Mrs. Buttercup's purposeful striding on Clematis montana legs, her pampas grass scarf and her tossed back clover head. The slanted angle of the dog's legs and the wind-wafted foreground grasses all indicate movement. At first I used marigold centres for the wheels but later found astrantia (Hattie's pincushion) a better substitute. Baby Buttercup is waving a single statice flower as a rattle!

Goat

While looking for pussy willow I discovered its poorer cousin—the goat willow. On discovering its name, and seeing the arch-like curve I immediately thought it would make a good neck for a goat. One of the many artemisias made his face and cotton grass covers his body which springs into action on legs of the underside segments of a wolf's bane leaf. His hooves are honeysuckle buds—and so are his purposeful horns!

The daffodil mini-skirted lady has not only lost her honeysuckle (halliana) budded balance but also her head! Her body is an honesty seedcase. Nipplewort bud is her nose and mouth, and her hair is Clematis Jackmannii seed head.

MISS GAILLARDIA ASH.

Miss Gaillardia Ash

Miss Gaillardia Ash was my second collage cartoon. Black, so our fashion designers tell us, is very smart and the young leaves of ash, when pressed, turn black. They make up Miss Ash's two-piece. Wouldn't it be nice if we could all find our own wardrobe as easily as this! Miss Ash wears a single "tippet" of pussy fur. When I made this picture I hadn't discovered that honeysuckle buds were suitable for making legs, and until then I used the very tiny leaves at the end of a Clematis montana frond. How useful this clematis is to me! Even the umbrella and one hand is constructed from this plant. Her handbag is a small ginkgo leaf with pussy willow clasp. The details of a face do not seem to be necessary in these cartoons. Why? I do not know, but her radiant red and orange face seems to "tell all" in a single gaillardia flower, embellished as it is with a hat of grey leaves and odd little bits of flowers.

"Say Cheese—Please—Miss Mouse"

The leaf pressing books are kept at the top of the stairs and, on my way to the bath, I spied a little dark leaf poking its head out of one of the books. Even at so early a stage it appeared to me like the head of a mouse! The leaf was so dry and brittle that in picking it up the edge of the leaf was accidentally nicked with my thumb nail. As so often happens, this "accident" became an advantage and made the mouse's mouth. Its needle sharp "nose" was the leaf end stem. By now the bath water had to be turned off as this picture was more important to me! His body is a prunus leaf pressed almost in the same way as for birds. Once again Clematis montana was used in a variety of ways including his smart bow tie and subtle bolt-hole in the grass stemmed wainscoting. Miss Mouse entwines her primrose stalk tail round his—of Clematis montana.

The Wise Owl

"Can you make an owl?" asked my publisher.
The request was a challenge, but on the train journey home the design and form that the body and head for an owl should take floated into my head like the very autumn leaves I was about to find in the garden. A scuffle amongst the wet leaves in my usual stamping ground produced two sycamore leaves. They only needed a week's pressing. Meanwhile an exploration of the pressing books revealed almost more variations of owl "feathers" than were needed. By simply placing the two leaves end to end the head and body were made. The wings were composed mainly by alternating the topside and underside of Senecio Greyii leaves. Honeysuckle buds made the pin feathers.
By placing a few rose petals on his chest it was possible to give it the necessary curve and sufficient lightness in tone to show up the broom petals and some grasses (which I found in a florist's) to give a speckled feather effect. Nearly all my store of bunny tail grasses were used to make up his fluffy plus-four trousers! Pressed pussy willow would have been more effective, but my publisher was so highly delighted with the result that he has used the design on the jacket of this book.

Pamela McDowall 7.12.70   Angry Ollie-Owl.

Two Little Fish

These two little fishes swam into life on Christmas Day evening. Each fish is made of a black parrot tulip petal which had been lying in the pressing book for three years. No cutting at all was made. The serrated edge to the petals is natural and, as the petals were dismantled, each to be pressed separately, so the small tear formed their fishy mouths. They breathe bubbles of life with gills of honesty —the lovely silver seedcase which does not need pressing.
Not wanting to miss a comedy show on television I carefully carried the as-yet-unstuck "pond weed" and fishes in with me to watch the programme. All went swimmingly until a burst of laughter from me blew the entire pond weed off the board! This is made up from bits of fern, asparagus, buttercup leaves and the dainty fennel.

Rabbits

Any small rounded brown leaf is suitable to make a rabbit's body. These leaves came from S. Africa. The "ears" are protea petals. Make use of any small leaf with an interesting serration to make "trees". Here is a grey leaf of Cineraria Diamond, wolf's-bane, santolina and bocconia poppy. Fennel is the "twiggy" tree.

"Three Little Maids from School"

The red anemone is one of the few red petals which I "trust" to retain its colour, and though they will eventually turn brown this is also a suitable colour for the girls' coats. It was while dismantling each flower (as the stigma is too lumpy to press and the stamens are too messy) that I noticed the irregular shape of some of the petals, as if they had little arms. As they lay side by side on the blotting paper I at once began whistling the song "Three little maids from school are we". I'd only to see the many varied colourings of the annual chrysanthemum and gaillardia as an immediate choice for a straw hat. Ideal too for a beach hat. Their satchels are part of a broom flower. One little girl has a delphinium petal scarf and their hands are pieces of buttercup leaves. Perhaps the slight angle of the petals and legs give the picture "life"—a standing stalk or grass all help to add movement.
This was my fifth cartoon.

"We Shop at Harrods . . ."

Here is an example of a leaf mal-pressed but, in this by mistake-on-purpose pressing, this prunus leaf picked up in November became another hat. Pressed in the same way as Farmer Barley Corn's sweet chestnut cap, as shown on page 70.

This lady favours the warmth of the pussy willow "fur" on her coat cuffs. She became slightly older than the other cartoon ladies simply by reversing the honeysuckle bud "leg" and making the thicker end the "thigh". Her little Yorkshire terrier type dog steals the picture as the wind blows into his silky clematis seed head face. For a Yorkshire terrier his tail is not correct, but the stalk was left on this clematis seed head for the body as it seemed so suitable.

Years of constant tread have caused this smartly clad lady to take a larger size in shoes by using the very end leaf-buds of cherry prunus, suitably curved. Her handbag is real aspen leaf "leather" and a gazania leaf's pointed end fastens it all together very smartly with what we must imagine is a good, firm sounding "clink-clunk"!

Pamela McDowall 25.2.71. 'We shop at Harrods' Mary Lee'.

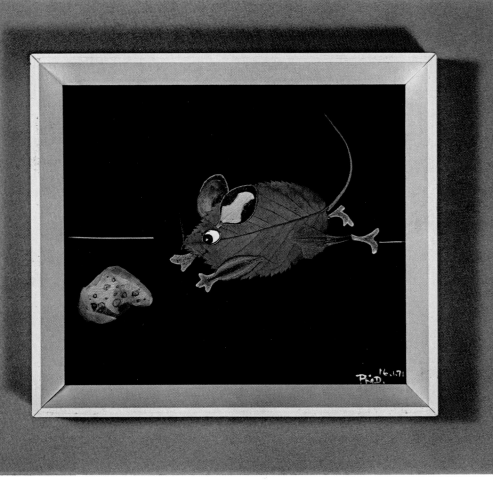

A Fat Mouse

A fat mouse—a greedy mouse! His tiny Nelly Moser clematis petalled legs and
Cineraria Diamond feet are barely able to bear his well nourished prunus leafed body.
Yellow freesia petal "cheese" is his staple diet and goal! His tail is a primrose stalk
and his ears are a Senecio Greyii leaf placed just inside another of the same.

A Daisy's Stretch at Dawn

Any curved stem forms a suitable basis for the female figure in foliage, e.g. a dancer or children running. This lovely curved stem of clematis at once evoked for me a graceful stretching daisy.

Aquarium

Self-sown honesty seedlings fill my garden and in spring the purple flower is left to seed. They are then tied up in bundles to hang upside down and their lovely silver seed cases left to dry in the tool shed. Their little shiny seed cases do not need pressing and, after peeling off the outer casings, are ready to use. To me, they always resemble the scales of herrings, and I had quite a game settling them down on to the black background without a cough or a sneeze ruining an hour's work. A few tulip petals have been added for fins and tails. To make the smaller schools of fishes the loose petals of rudbeckia and gazania (without its impossibly hard corolla) came in useful. A few ursinias make life-like sea urchins and with the ornamental grass lagurus (hare's tail) as pond weed all add to the marine life.

Pamela McDowall 25.3.71 *The Long Pull*

The Long Pull

The elongated shape of protea petals from the Cape suggested at once to me the
heads of baby birds, ducks and geese. Here are two grey geese having a tussle with
a resisting "worm". The former are made up of Senecio Greyii leaves with the tip of the
leaf turned back to indicate white tail feathers. I have used the end raspberry leaves
for the lower goose's wing. It's the feet that bring humour to the picture, each
"webbed foot" is a petal from a Tagetes erecta (African marigold). Rudbeckia, coreopsis
or gaillardia, all are equally suitable. Their feet are placed at an angle, to give the
running turned-in look. The straight part of the worm is a primrose stalk and the curly
bit is a vine tendril. Barren brome grass "whiskers" indicate excitement and movement.

"Artist and Model"

It was with some trepidation that I agreed to sit for my portrait, and I found no better cure for self-consciousness than for me to study the painter. So, while she portrayed me in oils I was preparing to cartoon her in petal foliage! Her stance was almost a foxtrot stride as she paced back and forth to the easel and this was clearly impressed on my mind. Her shoes had to be made from the very end leaves of the dark cherry prunus. From the same tree I made her body, and next the arms and legs from mimosa leaves (though willow would have been as suitable). Another smaller prunus leaf made her palette, and tiny pieces of buttercup and delphinium realized her paints. She holds in her Cineraria Diamond hand a nipped down pond grass as the paint brush. The easel is a piece of aspen poplar leaf, and the underside of gazania leaves makes the structure for it. The sleeves of the "model's" dress were strips of yellow tulip petal, twisted at the elbow to give the necessary gracefulness. The little expressive hand was very carefully chosen from a number of Cineraria Diamond leaf segments.

Pamela McDowall 14.2.71   The Artist and model.

Pamela McDowall 28.3.71.   The Rustle of Spring

The Rustle of Spring

In making this nest I was as anxious and diligent as any parent bird. Seeking, in my
own case, through every pressing book and on the floor for any stray bits and pieces to
compose the nest for Mrs. Black Bird's vociferous brood. Anything that was twig-like
went into this nest, from the bush shrub of Rhus Cotinus (royal purple), to fennel and
barren brome grass. The mother bird is perched on a twig of heather. Her beak is a
gazania petal, capable, one hopes, of a tussle with a vine tendril "worm". Protea petals
make suitable extenuated chicks' heads and silken pussy willow composes their
bodies. These "pussies" were gathered very early before the pollen had burst.

Farmer Barley Corn

I have described on page 46 how I came by these large chestnut leaves, which I had been given to create a soldier but somehow the idea did not work out. For several days two lay on my dressing table. Each time I went to brush my hair and get ready to go out I glanced at the crooked leaf to see what idea would come to me. Then suddenly, in less time than it took me to put in a hair grip, the top of the twisted leaf looked, not like a soldier, but a saucy farmer's cap! By now the horse chestnut leaf had moved up on the polished surface of the dressing table—to form his body. A sweet chestnut leaf was pushed up under the big leaf at a very slight angle and this gave Farmer Barley Corn his knicker-bockers. I knew now what these three big leaves were going to be and I went happily out to shop, planning as I walked along exactly what other bits and pieces of foliage were needed to complete the picture.

His Wellington boots were made from the top side of Senecio Greyii leaves.

I could hardly reach home quickly enough to finish the picture! Only the smaller details remained. This is when one must curb enthusiasm and not over-smother the collage picture.

Quickly I spied a tiny bit of aspen leaf and the dark topside made the "leather" patch for Farmer B.C.'s jacket. How glad I was that I found this tiny piece of leaf which had escaped from the pressing books to hide under the radiator and so escape the Hoover!

The previous summer I was sent some pink Japanese anemones to try out. They had turned out a little insignificant—however one petal made a quite suitable ear and it only remained for cotton grass (picked while on a visit to Otterburn) to give him his hair and moustache. A piece of red autumn leaf made his well-weathered nose and a curved stem of Clematis montana his gun.

Ideas for Heads, Bodies and Legs, etc.

Often it is only when one sees a leaf or flower that an idea is born. One day I saw a Clematis tangutica climbing over a pear tree and noticed how like Yorkshire terriers its silvery seed heads were. The owner generously said I could have them all, and in a flash I was up the tree and picked all I could reach! But here is a list of useful ideas to go on with——

ANTENNAE
    Vine tendrils
    Fuchsia stamens

BALLOON
    Honesty seedcase—inner silver

BALLS
    Mimosa, one "bobble"
    Buttercup bud—unopened

BIRDS
    Prunus leaves—autumn
    Clematis montana—very end of young leaves for flying crows
    Hornbeam—the leaf must have a pointed end for the beak
    Wych elm
    Plane—2 leaves ⎫ Owl
    Sycamore—2 leaves ⎭

BODIES
    Ash leaves
    Autumn leaf—open or folded
    Clematis montana—a single curved stem
    Clematis montana leaf—for butterfly body
    Senecio Greyii leaf
    Honesty—for fish scales
    Montbretia bud—for butterfly body

71

This is the very end leaf frond of Clematis montana. Nip off with your thumb nail one of the small leaves and you will have a very smart high-heeled court shoe.

BUBBLES
Honesty

BUTTERFLY
Sycamore "keys"—seed pods
Pansy (yellow and black)—petal wings
Tulip petal—for wings
Montbretia bud—for body
Delphinium petal—for wings
Freesia petal—for wings
Flanders poppy—for wings
Decorate "wings" with auricula flowers

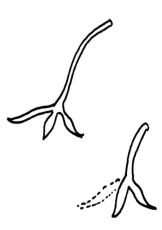

DOGS
Goat willow—silver female catkins
Pussy willow
Autumn leaves (small)—for dachshund
Clematis tangutica (seed heads)—for fur
Honeysuckle flower—for saluki

A single flower of honeysuckle can also be put to the same use as a boot or shoe. Just take out the stamens.

DRESS
Aspen silver—either side
Whitebeam—for coat
Daffodil trumpet—for skirt
Delphinium petals—for skirt
Freesia (yellow only)—for skirt
Ginkgo leaf—for ballet skirt
Trifolium repens purpurascens (lucky four-leaf clover)—for skirt
Sweet chestnut leaf—for gentlemen's plus-fours
Anemone *red* petals—for dress
Tulip petals—for skirt
Pussy willow—for scarf or tippet
Ornamental grass—for scarf, Lagurus ovatus or Bunny tail
Clover flower (half only)—for a collar

EARS

Senecio Greyii—for mouse or dog; and a folded small senecio leaf—
  for a human ear
"Keys" of sycamore (cut off the seed)—for rabbit ears
Chestnut leaf—for rabbit's ear
Two chestnut leaves—for rabbit's body

EYES

Honesty seeds
Buttercup bud—unopened
(*Or make your own in black ink or Biro on white paper*)

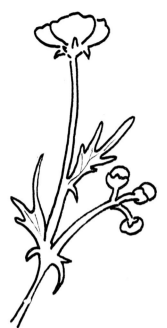

FEET

Centaurea gymnocarpa—for grey shoes
Cineraria Diamond—leaf segment for dog and mouse feet and paws,
  and human hands
Broom buds—for shoes
Laburnum bud—for shoes
Clematis montana leaves—very early end shoot leaves
Top side of aspen leaf for Wellington boots—if turned down at the
  tops—use a senecio leaf for each Wellington boot "top"
Japanese anemone (one petal for a human ear)

The leaves of the meadow buttercup make very "speaking" fingers and hands, and their little knobbly buds can be used for "noses".

FISH

Poppy petals
Tulip petals (Parrot tulip)
Honesty

FRILLS

Clover flower—half
Statice limonium sinuatum (dismantled)
Daisy (common) petals
Cineraria Diamond leaves

Meadow buttercup leaves for "hands" are most expressive.

73

HAIR
Cotton grass—hair and moustaches for elderly gentlemen
Tulip petal, Parrot variety
Ornamental grass—Hordeum jubatum, Fairy grass
Clematis tangutica—seed head
Pampas grass
Anemone alpina—seed head
Anemone Pulsatilla—seed head

HANDS
Cineraria Diamond leaf segment
Artemisia Absinthium (piece of) "Lambrook Silver"
Buttercup—small side leaves

HEADS
Clover
Daisy
Anthemis daisy
Autumn leaves—dark rounded
Honeysuckle—standard petal for saluki and dachshund's head and
   nose

HORIZONS
A single grass stem—for background hills

KITE
Ginkgo leaf

LEGS AND ARMS
Honeysuckle buds, best long "legged" variety is Lonicera halliana
Big white single petal of herbaceous daisy

NOSES, BEAKS
Buttercup buds
Melon pip
Birch leaf—yellow for owl's beak
Freesia—piece of yellow petal for duck's bill
Honeysuckle—for saluki dog's nose

74

NOTES (music)
  Very young buds of nipplewort

OWL
  Plane leaves—two
  Sycamore leaves—two
  Pampas grasses
  Ornamental grass—Bunny tail
  Broom petals for chest "feathers"—also grasses

SEA
  Delphinium petals

SHIPS AND SAILS
  Folded autumn prunus leaves
  Ginkgo leaf
  Willow leaf
  All slender autumn leaves

TAILS
  Grasses
  Barren brome grass
  Fairy grass—ornamental Hordeum jubatum
  Ornamental Lagurus ovatus (Bunny tail)
  Primrose stalks—for mice and dachshunds
  Gaillardia petal—for bird's feather tail

TEETH
  Turkey oak leaf—for crocodile

TIE
  Aronia erecta—use the small red leaves of this shrub

75

TREES

All grasses
Bocconia poppy (oak tree, both sides of leaf)
Wolf's-bane
Turkey oak (one leaf)
Briza minor—ornamental
Lagurus ovatus—ornamental Bunny tail grass
Ferns (tip of)
Wolf's-bane—underside
Echinops—both sides for fir trees
Senecio Greyii
Artemisia Absinthium
Asparagus in seed
Fennel
Barren brome grass
Fairy grass—ornamental Hordeum jubatum
Bocconia cordata (Plume poppy)—the leaves used alternately underside and top side make very lifelike "oak trees"

WORM

Vine tendril
Twisted primrose stalk

Ideas for Flower-Fashions

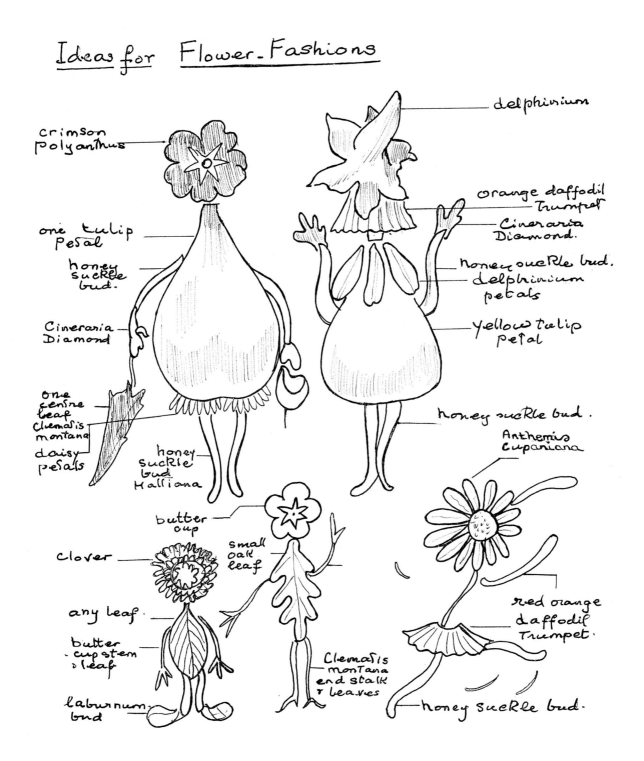

crimson polyanthus

delphinium

one tulip petal

honey suckle bud.

orange daffodil Trumpet

Cineraria Diamond.

honeysuckle bud.

delphinium petals

Cineraria Diamond

yellow tulip petal

one centre leaf Clematis montana

daisy petals

honey suckle bud Halliana

honey suckle bud.

Anthemis Cupaniana

butter cup

small oak leaf

clover

any leaf.

butter cup stem & leaf

laburnum bud

Clematis montana and stalk & leaves

red orange daffodil Trumpet.

honey suckle bud.

Any one for Jennis?

honesty

Cinerarea Diamond leaf segment

any stem.

mimosa

Clover

Honeysuckle Halliana

meadow buttercup leaf.

half an orange daffodil trumpet

Edge of underside of Cineraria Diamond leaf.

Honeysuckle Halliana bud

very early bud of honeysuckle.

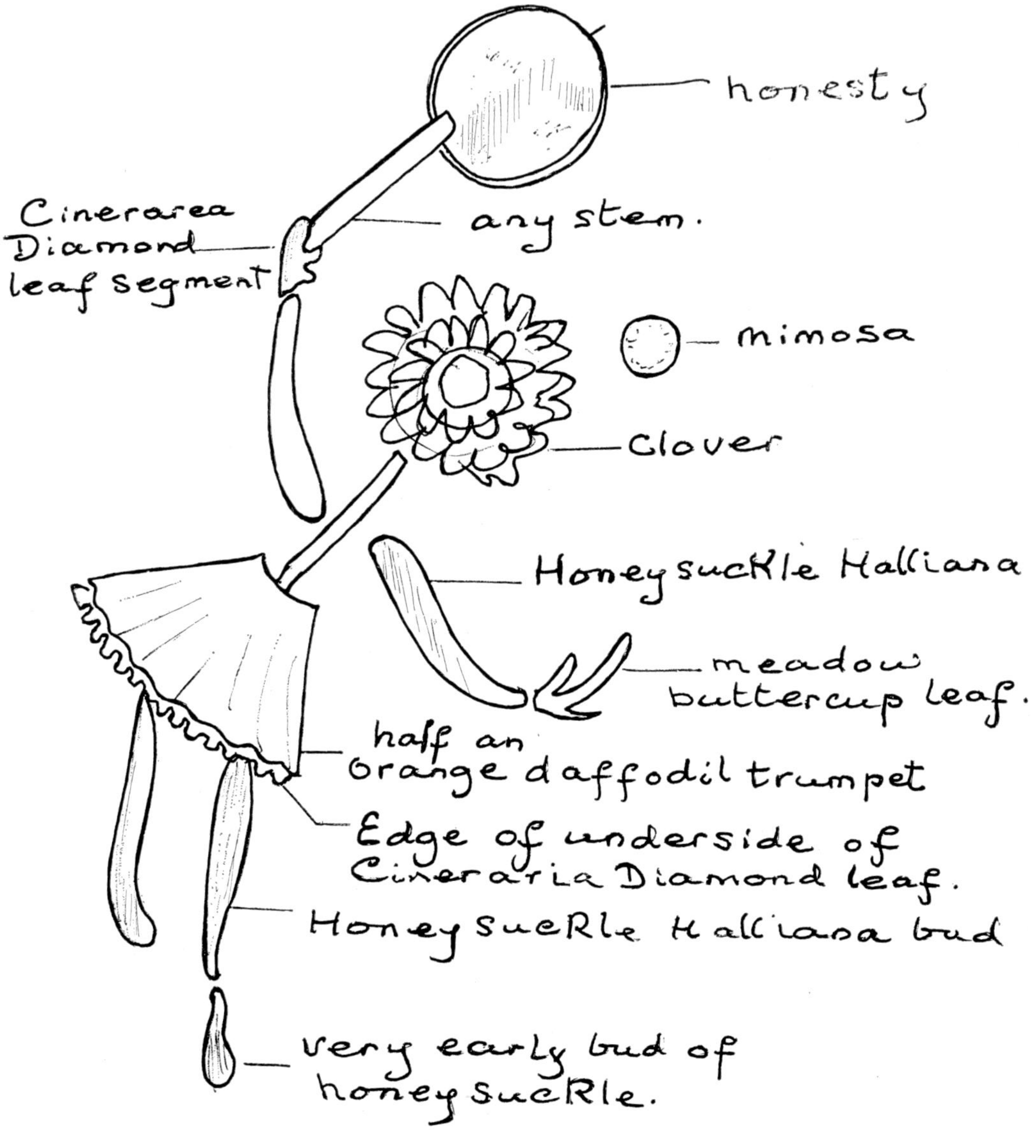

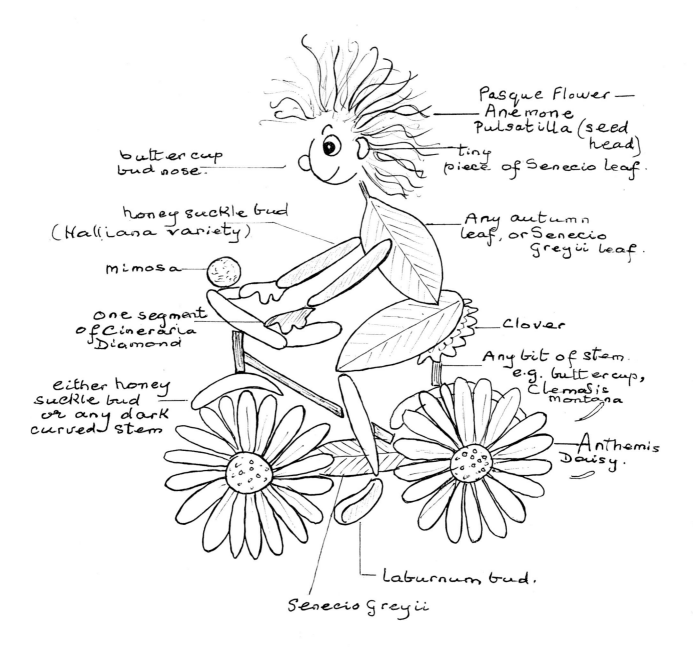

Pasque Flower —
Anemone
Pulsatilla (seed
head)

butter cup
bud nose.

tiny
piece of Senecio leaf.

honey suckle bud
(Halliana variety)

Any autumn
leaf, or Senecio
Greyii leaf.

mimosa

One segment
of Cineraria
Diamond

Clover

Any bit of stem.
e.g. buttercup,
Clematis
montana

either honey
suckle bud
or any dark
curved stem

Anthemis
Daisy.

Laburnum bud.

Senecio Greyii

4

Some Ideas for Things to Make

Matchboxes

These are ideal for a beginner and make very showy little bazaar gifts or "stocking-fillers" for Grandpas and Fathers! They are especially welcome, surely, if the design includes the elusive four-leafed clover and I like to feel the lucky clover matchbox never fails to light the garden bonfire! If you want a never ending supply of these, ask any alpine nursery for Trifolium repens purpurascens and you will find not only four-leafers but five and sometimes six! Pick them in full sun as they close up at sundown. I was very lucky to be sent one of these "tame" clovers by an early member of the press gang! But beware of slugs and human two-legged fanciers of this lovely, lucky, little plant.

Matchboxes come in several sizes. From the very small to the King Size. Cut out a piece of stiff paper, or thin white cardboard, to the exact size of the matchbox and stick on with Copydex, which is a rubberized adhesive solution (or similar non-inflammable glue). As the space is very limited, choose the flowers with care and remember especially that flowers grow from stalks (sometimes forgotten by flower-pressers!). It is these little stalks growing out from a fan-like base which make a balanced design. For these small designs, single loose petals can be composed into a "mock" flower, e.g. the yellow buds of freesias can become a "crocus", four delphinium petals a "periwinkle" and so on. Put in dainty grasses, the crimson summer-picked leaf of herb Robert or wild geranium, or the black lace-like flower and stems of hedge bedstraw. A place can often be found for any odd petals to create "mock" flowers on small objects such as matchboxes. It is now, when designing on so small a space, that you

80

Matchboxes

The one on the left is decorated with mimosa. At the base are petals of rudbeckia and two flowers of montbretia. The end of the box is decorated with a small spray of montbretia buds.

The flowers in the other design are made out of stray petals, the leaves at the base being meadow buttercup.

will find how glad you are so many of the stalks were picked and placed in the pressing books in a variety of curves. The stalks of the primrose are especially graceful when they have been grown in the shade and have been stretching out for light.

Lay the flowers on the design first, and when fully satisfied that the design balances, stick down the flowers, stalks and leaves.

To complete the matchbox decorate each end in coloured felts or flowers, and cover your design with adhesive plastic sheeting. Trim off the surplus sticky paper with scissors all round the matchbox.

Method of covering articles with transparent plastic

It is, of course, necessary to protect all pressed flower designs. Framed pictures are usually covered by glass but when we come to greeting cards, bookmarks and decorated matchboxes their protection is best provided by plastic material such as thin adhesive transparent sheeting which is readily available (I use Transpaseal or Fablon, but other makes are available and, of course, the criteria are that the material is as transparent as possible, is easy to handle, and, should we wish to stick the material down, is adequately adhesive; also prices and availability have to be considered).

The photos show how the sticky side of the adhesive plastic sheeting is pulled away from its protective wrapping and laid on the design— very carefully. Cut a piece a little wider than the matchbox and with a sharp finger nail free the top edge about a quarter of an inch and anchor it firmly on the matchbox with your fingers. At the same time, with the other hand, carefully peel the plain paper away from underneath and gently slide the top hand on to the material, smoothing it down firmly to avoid trapping any air bubbles. Only peel back a tiny bit at a time, while you press with the other hand. Have a trial run first with a small piece of the material on three or four pressed flowers. The petals may be drawn to the plastic by the presence of static electricity but this is best overcome by lowering and pressing the material quickly over the subject. But remember once a mistake is made, leave it, as it will be impossible to pull off the plastic without damaging all the flowers.

This shows a door finger-plate about to be covered with adhesive plastic sheeting. Peel away the protective plain wrapping with your thumb nails from the sticky paper. Cut the plastic a little bigger than the cardboard and design.

A design of wild flowers on a large matchbox is being covered with plastic. Free the top edge about $\frac{1}{4}$ in., and anchor it firmly on the design with your fingers. At the same time, with the other hand, carefully peel the plain paper away from underneath . . .

(Turn over to see the finishing stages.)

. . . gently sliding the left hand on to the material to smooth it down firmly and so avoid any air bubbles. Only peel a tiny bit at a time. As you tear away the backing paper, slowly draw your pressing hand towards you, keeping it as close as possible to the hand which is peeling the paper from underneath the adhesive plastic.

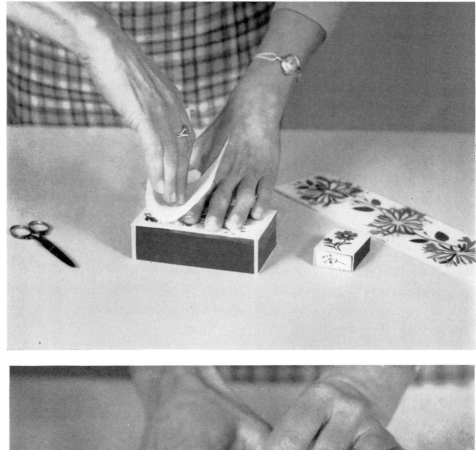

Trimming off the surplus sticky paper covering.

Greeting cards

These can be sent as a "Get Well" greeting card or as a Valentine as "a welcome message to a fair lady's ear"!

Anyone who is interested in the old meanings of flowers should buy a reprint of the earlier edition of *The Language of Flowers*. I have taken the list of flowers and their meanings from the original 1845 edition which I had the good fortune to be given for Christmas. It is greatly treasured. The list of meanings makes fascinated reading, and one can find much fun in choosing a suitable message by designing a little bouquet using pressed flowers. I suggest enclosing a little list of the flowers and their meanings on the back of the card.

Blank cards can be bought at any good stationer's. Stick the flowers on in the usual way and cover with plastic sheeting. Cut this a little bigger than the card itself so that it can be carried over the edge to the inside.

A Greeting Card

Montbretia buds, honeysuckle and tiny florets of blue statice limonium sinuatum (sea lavender) give a "pillow" for the yellow-and-black pansy to rest on. Also included are the creeping buttercups and buds, pond primula and a small piece of the shade-loving Tiarella Wherryi, not forgetting two florets of ground elder and along the base Clematis Viticella and a spike of barren brome grass.

Greetings

An anthemis daisy is surrounded by nine honesty seed cases. Interspersed behind these are the smallest (underside up) leaves of echinops. They were picked in August. Spraying out are pieces of fennel, a fine ornamental grass and pampas grass.

Engagements

A five-leafed clover and stem makes the body of the little lady bearing in her honeysuckle bud arm a posy of dainty leaves, hedge bedstraw, Hattie's pincushion and petals of delphinium. Her hat is made of two creeping buttercup petals and a small piece of ornamental grass is a "feather".

Notes

The bars of music are made of Clematis montana stalks. The "apology" for the notes of music are buds off the nipplewort weed! Below this is hedge bedstraw.

Best Wishes

The yellow-and-black pansy was my starting point here. The line of stalks of the other flowers is important to make the spray effective. Heuchera, buttercup, astrantia (Hattie's pincushion), clover and part of a fuchsia. Silver leaves are Artemisia Absinthium Lambrook Silver.

All are protected by adhesive plastic sheeting.

Greetings

Engagements

Notes

Best
Wishes

Pamela McDonald.   " I 'leaf' it all So You — dear Valentine"

Valentine

"I 'leaf' it all to you."

A Valentine using the underside and topsides of very small leaves, both autumn and summer. Only the centre "heart" is cut out from a piece of red paper from an old Christmas card.

The "gentleman" leaf and his intended lady need no heads; the sentiments they are expressing are in their "leafy hearts".

Calendars

Here is a design for a calendar. The pressed flowers are covered with a transparent plastic sheet and sealed round on the first mount before final fixing on to a suitable outer mount. There are three pieces in all, one white (for the designs) and two of two brown tones, one matching the flower vase which is cut out of the same piece of coloured paper. The vase can be made of material such as tweed, chinz, or a paper material which looks like a wicker basket, such as a suitable wallpaper sample. Be sure when sticking down the material to put only the tiniest amount of "sticky" on all single petals, leaves and stalks as it is essential, when the design is to be covered in plastic sheet, to ensure that *no petal is loose* when the sticky paper is rolled over, as once in position it cannot be removed to adjust a petal.

Here is a list which might help the reader choose wisely his message for the "dear one"!

ANEMONE	Forsaken	HONESTY	Fascination
ASH LEAF	Grandeur	HONEYSUCKLE	Can be generous devoted affection
ASPEN	Lamentation	JONQUIL	I desire a return of affection
BRAMBLE LEAF	Envy or lowliness		
BROOM	Humility, neatness	KING-CUPS	Desires of riches
CELANDINE	Joys to come		
CLEMATIS	Mental beauty	LABURNUM	Forsaken, Pensive beauty
CLOVER (white)	Think of me	LADY'S SLIPPER	Haughtiness or Capricious beauty
CLOVER (four-leaf)	Be mine		
COREOPSIS	Always cheerful	LARKSPUR	Lightness, levity
COREOPSIS ARKANSAS	Love at first sight	LAVENDER	Distrust
DAFFODIL (big yellow)	Regards	PANSY	You occupy my thoughts
DAFFODIL	Chivalry		
DAISY (common)	I will think of it	POLYANTHUS (crimson)	The heart's mystery
DAISY (garden)	I share your sentiments	QUAKING GRASS	Agitation
		RUDBECKIA	Justice
DAISY (ox-eye)	Patience or Penitence	TENDRILS	Ties
FUCHSIA	Taste, or Hopeless not heartbroken	WILLOW	Forsaken
GERANIUM	Be comforted	WOLF'S-BANE (leaf)	Misanthropy

Butterflies

Making your very own butterflies to decorate your pictures, be they for large or small, can be great fun. There is such a vast range of colours in petals to choose from to make their wings and once started on these you will find it difficult to stop! I owe the inspiration to a keen flower-presser from Lochgoilhead in Argyllshire, whose picture looked so dainty with its one little "moth" made from two sycamore "keys". I saw this in Edinburgh when I was invited to judge an exhibition of pressed flower pictures and have developed the idea in my own way.

From this first dainty Scottish "moth" grew my own type of butterfly! Tulip petals are a "must". Do not worry about the saucer-like shape of each fresh tulip petal as it is dismantled. When placed individually into the pressing books, they dry out perfectly flat, and although the inner, more curved petal may split half way up the centre, this is an advantage. Use each complete split half for a butterfly's two top "wings". The red-and-yellow variety is very pretty, almost like shot-silk. Decorate the two lower petal-wings with the somewhat startling dominance of auricula or from parts of the lower striking yellow-and-black pansy petals. Sycamore "keys" make good top "wings" and rose petals can be added for the lower ones. Pansy, delphinium, yellow freesia and the already well marked by nature Flanders poppy are all very effective as wings.

Very life-like "bodies" for your butterfly can be made from any curved stalk, or seed box of a young fuchsia flower. The half-open early bud of montbretia, a twisted Clematis montana leaf or very young prunus leaves can all be used. These give a most natural bend in the butterfly's body. For the head use a buttercup bud or centre part of a fuchsia.

The fuchsia's stigma make ideal antennae, also the tendrils off a grape vine. If you cannot find any of these near you, a "whisker" off the barren brome grass or barley ear makes an ideal "feeler", or a bristle of the broom in the brush cupboard.

The possibilities and fun are endless and I'm sure someone soon will make a dragonfly with wings of honesty! Yes? Try!

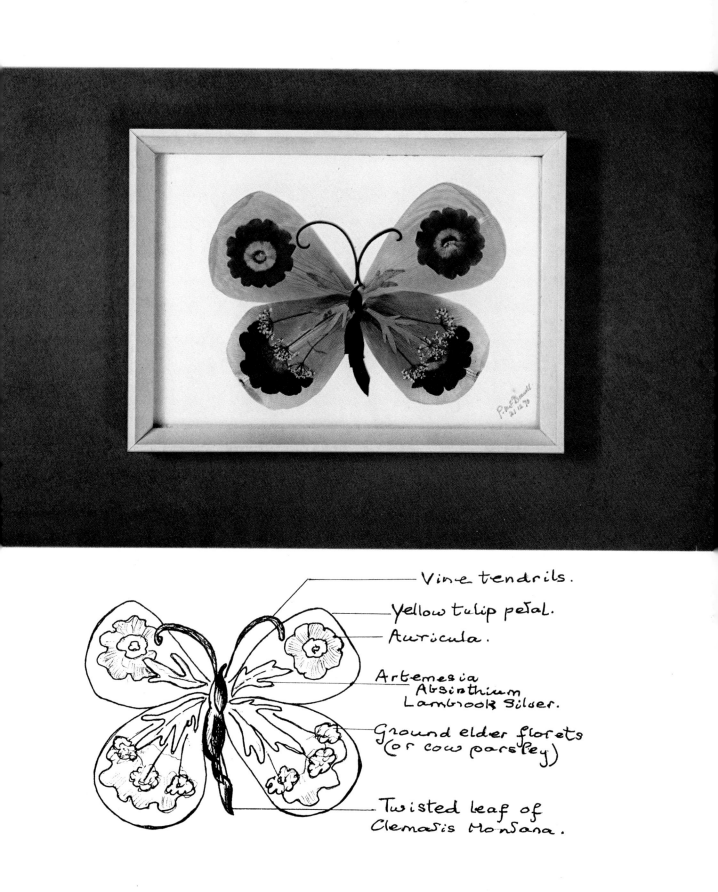

Vine tendrils.

Yellow tulip petal.

Auricula.

Artemesia
Absinthium
Lambrook Silver.

Ground elder florets
(or cow parsley)

Twisted leaf of
Clematis Montana.

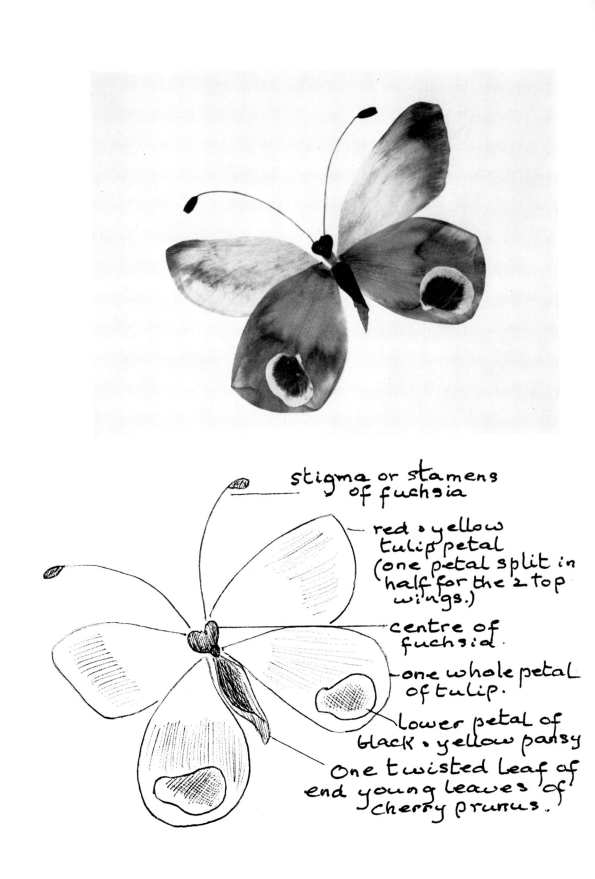

stigma or stamens
of fuchsia

red & yellow
tulip petal
(one petal split in
half for the 2 top
wings.)

centre of
fuchsia.

one whole petal
of tulip.

lower petal of
black & yellow pansy

One twisted leaf of
end young leaves of
cherry prunus.

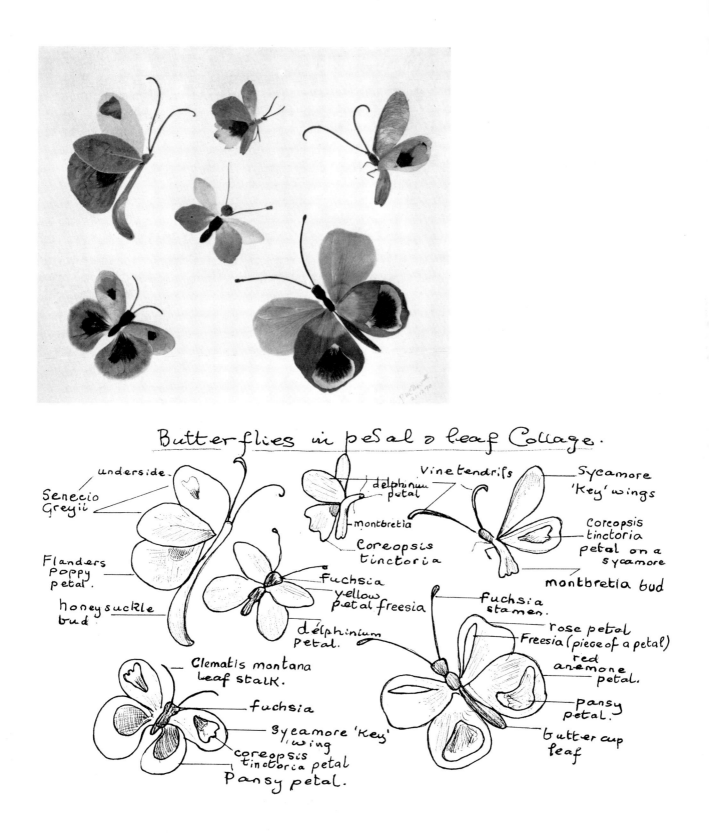

Butterflies in petal & leaf Collage.

underside

Senecio Greyii

Flanders Poppy petal.

honeysuckle bud

Vine tendrils

delphinium petal

montbretia

Coreopsis tinctoria

Sycamore 'Key' wings

Coreopsis tinctoria petal on a sycamore

montbretia bud

Fuchsia

Yellow petal freesia

delphinium Petal.

Clematis montana leaf stalk.

fuchsia

Sycamore 'Key' wing

coreopsis tinctoria petal

Pansy petal.

Fuchsia stamen.

rose petal

Freesia (piece of a petal)

red anemone petal.

Pansy petal.

buttercup leaf

Table mats

Table mats are very easy to make and are useful too for flower vases to stand on, and decorative when not in use. Keep them out of direct sunlight to retain their colour as long as possible.

Ask a glazier to cut a piece of glass of either 24 oz. or 32 oz. thickness to, say, sizes 7″ × 7″, 6″ × 6″ or 5″ × 5″. This weight of glass will take the heat of a not *too* hot dinner plate. You will need pieces of thick cardboard cut to these sizes of glass, and for backing use a piece of tweed from an old skirt or a square of felt.

Stick the backing to the cardboard and decide on what colour background to use to lay out your flower design. All colours of paper can be bought in sheets at stationers. Grey leaves and white flowers show up well on a crimson background. Yellows, whites and grey leaves look lovely on a black background.

Having stuck down the design of flowers, place on the glass and bind the edges of glass, cardboard and back together with the most suitable colour of adhesive tape. This operation is more easily done if you place the mat just over the edge of the table.

Table Mats

A black background is ideal for showing up the large black-and-yellow pansy and buttercups (and buds). The common daisy and dainty ground elder florets have been touched up with white poster paint before laying out the design. The underside of a Cineraria Diamond leaf is in the left-hand corner.

A table mat decorated with buttercups, limnathes, clover, cow parsley, daisies and celandine, and in the corner one black-and-yellow pansy. The celandines will go white in a few months but as they are on a black background they will still show up well. Pieces of leaf from the lovely silver-leaved Artemisia Absinthium, Lambrook Silver, fill in any too obvious spaces.

A white background table mat with hedge bedstraw, five delphinium petals, mimosa, buttercups, montbretia (in bud), clover (with their centre whorls touched up with white poster paint), tiny herb Robert leaves, honeysuckle and florets of ground elder, all held together with a four-leafed clover—Trifolium repens purpurascens—placed above the yellow-and-black pansy.

Door finger-plates

Door finger-plates can be made for as little or as much as you wish, depending on whether the pressed flower design is covered with transparent panels of perspex (which can be purchased at any hardware store), or by simply covering the design with the transparent sticky adhesive paper as already mentioned earlier for covering matchboxes.

If the door finger-plate design is to be covered with perspex panels it is best to buy these panels first, as they sometimes vary in length, and then cut out the cardboard. They are usually 10″ × 3″. However, the advantage of covering the design in the sticky transparent paper is that one can make the panel any length or breadth one wishes and it costs very little.

The method is to cut a piece of cardboard to the required size and position your design of pressed flowers. As the space is very limited, stalks should play a leading part if the design is to be well balanced. Make a neat, compact and interesting base and let the stalks and flowers radiate and curve upwards. Any little side spaces can be filled in with dainty grasses, buttercup buds, nipplewort or hedge bedstraw. Stick down the design of flowers in the usual way and place the perspex or the sticky transparent paper over the design. In each case, however, the edges must be sealed round. Use adhesive tape for the perspex panel, and when using the transparent sticky paper cut this out about $\frac{1}{2}$″ bigger than the cardboard so that it can be sealed round over the edges. A centre screw-hole either end, to fix the panel to the door, is all that is then required.

If the finger-plate is fixed to a sunny door it is best to use non-fading materials, such as clover and grasses. Nevertheless if the flowers do fade after a year or so they can easily be replaced if under perspex by taking off the surrounding binding, and if the flower was fixed by the latex type adhesive, this is soon rubbed off with a *clean* finger!

Embedding flowers in plastic

It was while staring into a gift shop window that I saw a little sea-horse and also goldfish staring back at me from a clear plastic cube. The thought occurred to me: "Why not put in pressed flowers—as paperweights, door finger-plates or plaques in plastic—but how?"

Door Finger-plates

Three door finger-plates using small light-coloured flowers or lotus petals, for instance in the example on the left, five loose anthemis petals were laid on five loose delphinium petals to create a mock periwinkle. The one in the centre shows clovers with their centre whorls accentuated with white poster paint; the grass is one of the bedstraws.
On the right is a contrasting design of leaves and ornamental grass heads. I took the leaves from a potted fern and in my enthusiasm totally denuded it of its foliage.

(*Far left*) The yellow-and-black pansy placed at the base of a door finger-plate design gives it a strong, dominant start, especially as the pansy is laid on top of delphinium petals. The stalks of buttercups, egg-and-bacon plant, pond grass, montbretia, bunny tail and briza minor grass take one's eye to the top flower, which in this plate is an eschscholzia which because of its very paleness will not be used again for pressing.

Door Finger-plates

(Far right)
Here is a design of four daffodils on a black background. The
trumpets and petals have been pressed and dried separately and then
reassembled. A buttercup's half-open bud supplants the daffodil's
ovary, which is too hard and knobbly to press. Do not press the stalk
of the daffodil but use any silver stem. I was fortunate in finding a
few very thin gazania leaves and using the underside of these for the
stalks.

(Centre)
A door finger-plate using delphinium (or blue larkspur), brought
down to size by sticking each small bud and flower on to a stalk of
Anthemis Cupaniana or stem of Artemisia Absinthium and adding
leaves *not* of the delphinium but similar in shape, earth- or pig-nut
and Artemisia Absinthium.

(Right)
Any loose petals or "leftovers" are useful to make mock flowers.
Montbretia, pressed while in bud in curves, is lovely arranged in the
confined space of a door finger-plate and so are the little black-and-
white striped buds of Clematis Viticella as shown here to fill in any
spaces and guide the eye upwards to the top flowers, which in this
case are a Welsh poppy, buttercup, ursinia and annual
chrysanthemum. The base is composed of seven loose petals of
sunburst.

Flowers in Plastic

These are examples of the numerous ways pressed flowers can be encased in plastic to create pretty paperweights or just attractive objects in themselves. The two on the right were cast in a rubber mould, while the remainder were made by using the kit described in the text. The anthemis on the black background was made in a large ash tray (the dew-drops are air bubbles which should have been excluded but they are highly effective additions to the attractive design), while the delphinium was made in a tumbler; these, as well as some of the other examples, were made by ten-year-old Lucy Foxell. I myself made the heart-shaped example at the far right of the top row, and all the examples in the bottom row.

The only person I knew who did wonders with materials was the portrait sculptor and artist, Charles Stitt. It was his flat's interior décor of golds and brown which had inspired me to create Plate 14 in *Pressed Flower Pictures*, two years ago.

To my inquiry about plastic and putting things into it, other than a sea-horse, and did he think it possible to embed pressed flowers into plastic, he said "Yes. I should think so", and a torrent of explicit instructions poured like molten plastic down the phone on how I was to do it—but—with what? Soon, he said, he would come down and show me. But when? Pinning down an artist to a day for a real session for instruction on my idea of embedding flowers in the plastic polyester resin was the biggest problem of all. But the great day did arrive, and, stuffed as we were with turkey and mince pies, a demonstration happened.

Now truly, I am the biggest fool ever with anything that needs essentials such as making a mould. I also get equally blank in mind when photography is described to me—though I love taking photos—but the intricacies of it are as complicated as if I had been asked to handle a space-ship and take off to the moon. It's the same with lino-cuts, the ability to "think backwards"—if you understand my meaning—being quite impossible for me! I also get equally panicky and behave like a hysterical hen if asked the age-old problem—"If a herring and a half cost three ha'pence . . .", so you can see that I was a somewhat timid pupil when Charles was about to show me how to mix the chemicals and how to make a mould. I can therefore assure you that if I can master it, you can too, for it is, oh! so simple.

Perhaps it should be explained at the start that the principle is to make a solid block of polyester resin, a crystal clear plastic in which the pressed flower is embedded. It is built up in layers, a hardener being stirred into the resin before it is poured into a mould. The mould can either be a container such as a pyrex dish or a baking tin or a china bowl, or a special rubber mould of any shape can be made by using a silastomer. I have tried both methods. Using basic materials obtained from a supplier of sculptor's materials and following the instructions sheet provided, we made a mould from a heart-shaped baking tin and this was used to set a flower-design in plastic to form an attractive paperweight.

The other method was even easier, as I bought a kit called "Plasticraft" which is obtainable at good toy shops. This kit contains all the necessary chemicals, colouring dyes, various shaped moulds in a ceramic block, "findings" for making cuff links, ear-rings, etc., and full instructions.

It is, as I have said, a very straightforward process which can give wonderful results, provided the instructions are meticulously followed. My advice is to start with very simple designs, probably a single flower (though don't forget the stalk) such as a pansy, a gaillardia, an anthemis, or, although I am usually opposed to red as a choice, Lobelia cardinalis, but soon one can be more adventurous and place flowers at different levels (allowing the resin to set in layers) which gives the design a lovely feeling of floating in space.

It is worth noting that flowers which do not retain their colour when pressed, lose their colour immediately when placed as fresh flowers in clear plastic. An example is the love-in-the-mist in the illustration below, and similar results are obtained from coloured roses and forget-me-nots. Buttercups, however, keep their colour and so do pressed delphiniums.

Paperweight

This half-spherical paperweight made of clear plastic contains a fresh love-in-the-mist. I don't press these flowers as they turn a dirty brown, but here the colour of the fresh flower turned to pure white and the whole thing is most effective against a red background.

105

Four flowers set in clear plastic. *Top*, some common daisies on a blue background; *centre*, a polyanthus (set too close to the edge of the plastic so it is a little distorted in this photograph), and a buttercup; *below*, two helichrysums (everlasting flowers) of a delicate pink and white with strands of fine grass beneath and set against a dark-blue background. All these examples were made by Lucy Foxell, aged ten.

Bookmarks

Attractive bookmarks can be made using pressed flowers and grasses. It is worth remembering that there is a wide choice of flowers to select for bookmarks as they will spend most of their useful lives in a closed book which is the ideal condition in which to preserve the colours, hidden away from the light. Obviously it is very important that such markers are not in the least bulky for that would damage the binding of a book. I am experimenting with four methods and readers may have other ideas of materials which can be effectively used. Anyway here are some suggestions for creating bookmarks as presents for friends or gifts for sale at bazaars:

Stiff-paper backing

Cut a piece of stiff drawing paper a little longer than the average depth of a book, say 9 inches, and simply stick the pressed flowers on it. As space is very limited long grasses are especially suitable—either the ornamental grasses, briza minor, fairy grass, Agrostis elegans or the very fine dainty grass Agrostis pulchella and the Lagurus ovatus known as bunny or hare's tail. These ornamental grasses can all be grown from a packet of seed listed in any seed catalogue. They can also be found growing wild in hot countries.

When the design is stuck down, cover over with Transpaseal or a similar plastic sheet in the same way as the matchbox described earlier.

Plastic backing

For this method I use Polyglaze which is a flexible clear plastic which is sold as a substitute for glass, for instance as garden cloches. It can be bought in a roll and cut with a sharp knife or scissors.

Here again the plastic is cut to the required shape and the design laid upon it, remembering that the flowers or grass or whatever

Bookmark

Stiff paper has been used for the background. The design is made up of ornamental grasses, briza minor, barren brome grass, fairy grass, Agrostis elegans, Agrostis pulchella, the Lagurus ovatus (bunny or hare's tail), the buds of nipplewort and the underside of one gazania leaf.

107

Bookmarks

Five bookmarks, showing varied designs and two different treatments. The first two on the left are made on a clear plastic backing covered with an adhesive plastic sheeting so that they are transparent (though they have been photographed against a white card to make the designs stand out against the green background). The other three are backed with ribbon and protected by adhesive plastic sheeting.

From left to right:

1. A design built up from a base of three rudbeckia petals. The other flowers are buttercups and clover, with segments of leaves of Artemisia Absinthium, Lambrook Silver.

2. Another design in which buttercups predominate, but also including heuchera, single petals of gaillardia, goose grass and herb Robert.

3. A brown ribbon is used to back a design of celandines and the silver leaves of Artemisia Lambrook Silver.

4. Here the design is made from the buds of Clematis Viticella and nipplewort against the background of a white ribbon.

5. Leaves of sycamore picked in very early growth and a segment of a grass which grows in my goldfish pool.

material is used can be viewed from both sides. Keep the design well spaced and balanced, and ensure that the adhesive is used very sparingly. I then cover the whole with Transpaseal, cutting out the latter a little larger than the Polyglaze to allow for inaccuracy when pressing down; one can always trim off the surplus afterwards. To make a neat finish cut each end with pinking scissors and add a satin bow if you wish.

Ribbon backing

Here the same technique is followed as for the other backing materials, including the use of the adhesive transparent plastic sheeting. The ones I made required a very steady hand, while moving and sticking down the wiry little stalks of clematis was like playing spillikins. They took about an hour each, but as a compensation they are wonderfully flexible and as thin as paper which makes them very nice to use and therefore very successful.

Film negative backing

The advantage of this unusual type of backing are that the whole is light, thin, flexible, transparent and can be finished without the use of adhesive plastic sheeting which is not ideal.

The examples I have seen, some of which are shown opposite, were made by a correspondent in South Africa—and highly professional they are. The designs are exquisitely executed.

The principal material required for each bookmark is a double sheet of ordinary 35mm film from which the emulsion has been removed. Ideally the film should be obtained in wholesale quantities (and, what is more important, at wholesale prices) from a government surplus store or manufacturer's stock which was faulty or has exceeded the recommended period of its normal life as a film, but failing that standard film can be bought. To remove the emulsion it should be soaked for several hours in washing soda and hot water, after which the emulsion will come away by scraping with a knife and wiping with a cloth (alternatively, and this seems to be a less laborious method, I am told it can be put into the usual photographic fixative and washed). The result will be a clear plastic strip of just the right width

Bookmarks

These exquisite bookmarks came from the Cape. The compact yet elegant designs are created with pressed flowers, grasses and reeds. The transparent film is bound with silk cord and the first three from the left are backed with a silk-type ribbon. The one on the right is unbacked and uses blue lobelia flowers. Personally, I have not yet experimented with pressing lobelia to test whether it retains its colour, though I recognize that as bookmarks are not exposed to light there is a greater freedom of choice of flowers.

and thickness, with holes perforated to permit binding of the two pieces together. However most film will turn out a pale blue colour and to get a completely colourless strip a fine grain positive safety film should be used, if obtainable.

It can be seen that there are technical difficulties in producing such bookmarks, which can be either completely transparent or contain a ribbon or coloured paper as a backing to the flower arrangement, yet the result is extremely effective if the design is well executed.

There are so many other possibilities besides the ones I have described here. You can make your own presents, help out at bazaars and sales with a "pressed flower" stall, and so on. Children can have a marvellous time—look at the examples made by a ten-year-old on pages 103 and 106—and convalescents can make small things like bookmarks and greeting cards while sitting up in bed. You will find yourself looking at leaves and flowers in quite a different way: not just as something to pick and arrange in a vase, but as creative material which you can use in paperweights, calendars, gay cartoons and graceful pictures for your walls. A large red tulip petal makes a marvellous body for Humpty Dumpty sitting on his wall, three pansies make a dear old lady—there is no end to the possibilities. Just remember not to overpick, not to waste your flowers and grasses. Most of the examples shown in this book came by accident, very few of them were planned—and none of the designs needed to be drawn in advance.

A bookmark on white cardboard comprising montbretia buds and grass with a freesia pressed in star-fashion as a base.